Followership

Faithful Following in an Age of Confusion

Steven R. Timmermans

WIPF & STOCK · Eugene, Oregon

FOLLOWERSHIP
Faithful Following in an Age of Confusion

Copyright © 2022 Steven R. Timmermans. All rights reserved. Except for brief quotations in critical publications or reviews, no part of this book may be reproduced in any manner without prior written permission from the publisher. Write: Permissions, Wipf and Stock Publishers, 199 W. 8th Ave., Suite 3, Eugene, OR 97401.

Wipf & Stock
An Imprint of Wipf and Stock Publishers
199 W. 8th Ave., Suite 3
Eugene, OR 97401

www.wipfandstock.com

PAPERBACK ISBN: 978-1-6667-5966-2
HARDCOVER ISBN: 978-1-6667-5967-9
EBOOK ISBN: 978-1-6667-5968-6

12/21/22

Scriptures taken from the Holy Bible, New International Version®, NIV®. Copyright © 1973, 1978, 1984, 2011 by Biblica, Inc.™ Used by permission of Zondervan. All rights reserved worldwide. www.zondervan.com The "NIV" and "New International Version" are trademarks registered in the United States Patent and Trademark Office by Biblica, Inc.™

Followership

"As a diversity, equity, and inclusion leader, I appreciate the authentically transparent approach in this book. Each chapter drew me in, compelling me to reflect upon my understanding of followership as experienced throughout my life and in observations of others. This book will both challenge and equip you to be a better follower and leader within and beyond the workplace, across human differences, and throughout different life stages."

—**RHAE-ANN BOOKER**, vice president of diversity, equity, and inclusion, University of Michigan Health-West

"Timmermans has a history of effective leadership in multiple organizations; based on this history, he could have written yet another leadership book. Instead, he gives his attention to the vital corollary of leadership—the wisdom, even when in leadership, of following well. This is a wise and winsome book, with lessons for followers and leaders alike."

—**CLAUDIA BEVERSLUIS**, professor and provost emerita, Calvin University

"I've read many books on leadership. But Steven Timmermans is the only author I know who has written on 'followership.' And this is not about old, hierarchical forms of submission. Rather, Steve illumines what it means to be a committed, discerning follower in today's church and society. Here's a refreshing, insightful look at a topic no one writes about but everyone practices: following."

—**WESLEY GRANBERG-MICHAELSON**, general secretary emeritus, Reformed Church in America

"Any book authored by Steve Timmermans, a respected educational and denominational leader, has my attention. Here readers will find a refreshing contrast to the emphasis typically found in leadership literature on the role of the individual leader; instead, Timmermans offers fresh thinking and an upside-down-kingdom perspective on how Spirit-led followers can contribute to individual and societal well-being amidst the complexities of our day."

—**KAREN A. LONGMAN**, professor of higher education, Azusa Pacific University

"As a president of an academic institution I read extensively in the literature about leadership. Now I wish I could also have read Steve Timmermans' wise book. He not only shows how effective leadership must be grounded in discerning followership—he does it in a winsome manner that draws on compelling life experiences!"

—**RICHARD J. MOUW**, president emeritus, Fuller Theological Seminary

This book is dedicated to Barb Bosscher Timmermans who has faithfully lived out her marriage pledge to help develop God's gifts in me, as I have sought to do the same for her. In addition, the suggestions and encouragement in this book are dedicated to our children—Katie and Ben, Paul, Yainieabeba and Sam, Becca and Abel, Jess and Christopher, Getenet and Bethelihem, and Fekadu—with our prayer that they may follow faithfully.

Contents

Acknowledgements | ix
Introduction | xi

1   Welcome to ~~Leadership~~ Followership | 1
2   Following the Leader—The Role of Gender | 14
3   Following the Leader—The Role of Culture and Race | 25
4   Following the Leader—Into Adulthood | 36
5   Following the Leader—In the Workplace | 46
6   Following the Leader—In Marriage and Family Life | 59
7   Following the Leader—In Society | 68
8   Following the Leader—In Church and Christian Community | 85
9   Faithful Followership | 100

Bibliography | 111

Acknowledgements

I'm grateful to Marcia Vermaire Bosscher whose frequent encouragement, many suggestions, and helpful critique of this book in all of its many iterations kept me writing and ultimately allowed me to share my thoughts in the best possible ways. I'm grateful, too, for the First CRC's men's book/spiritual accountability group for reading the manuscript and providing me with invaluable advice as well. Finally, thanks to all of those on the campuses and other settings where I've served who helped me to listen well and follow faithfully.

Introduction

Every generation seems to declare their times are challenging, whether because of war, economic uncertainties, or leadership. If we go back to the entry of Jesus into Jerusalem just days before his crucifixion, we imagine the streets lined with followers waving palm branches, yet we know they were confused and hopeful about all the wrong things. This generation and these times are not an exception. In the second and third decades of this century, we've seen a pandemic that left us quarreling about public protocols while the death toll continued to grow, divisiveness in the social glue called democracy, unparalleled aggression toward a neighboring country in Europe, a backlash of racism after the United States' first black president. The list goes on.

We look to our leaders during times like these. Will they inspire us to find unity? Will they introduce policy and legislation to set new boundaries for guns, actions, and discourse? Will they model civility and care of the neighbor? What are we to do?

Yes, we look to our leaders, but we also need to look at ourselves: we who follow the leaders. While we might seek to place blame on leaders for these unsettling times, we each should accept our share of the blame. At times, we're like a herd of cats, each going his or her own way. At other times, we become so affixed to a cause or a person, we lose all objectivity.

Why are these times so unsettling? My belief is that postmodernism opened the door to relativity—that all truths are

Introduction

worthy—and the Internet has provided unequaled dissemination of this incredible heterogeneity of ideas and belief. Thus, we have ceased following one truth in more or less unison and have scattered in individualist directions. Facts—especially scientific facts—seem to be waning in importance, as people decide about public health measures based on what they find on the Internet that confirms their beliefs, sometimes in direct opposition to scientific facts. In other words, we have begun to follow our own biases. So, if a given leader reflects my bias, I follow him or her. Holding tightly to my specific belief about a group of people, I can justify my own discrimination and fail to even consider systemic undercurrents.

Given my former roles in higher education, I care about young adults who are launching into this stormy sea of subjectivity. But it's not just young adults; it's all of us. Institutions such as local school boards, community library boards, and even some churches that have sought to find unity among diverse people are being challenged. I fear the ultimate result: retreat into homogeneous relationships disconnected from relationships to government, church, and other institutions. The result becomes a balkanization of life.

Every generation needs to learn how to live in this postmodern, pluralistic society. Reading books and going to seminars on leadership is insufficient. Trying to turn back the clock will not work. Each of us needs to understand how to work for a Muslim boss. We need the insight and sensitivity to enter into and sustain a marriage. We need to shed old paradigms that worked a generation or two ago and bring deep discernment into the voting booth. We need to follow Christ in the church, within institutions and throughout communities formed by people, all with feet of clay.

In short, among the swirling truths and non-truths that bombard us, we need keen discernment to follow leaders who hold universal truths, to follow causes that reflect transcendent faithfulness, to follow Christ in all things.

In the following chapters my desire is to help you explore followership—including examination of the dimensions of gender

Introduction

and culture. After the first three chapters, I invite you to consider followership in the development stage of young adulthood, in the workplace, in marriage and family life, in society, and in the church and Christian community. Hopefully, by the time you reach the last chapter, you will be able to appreciate my summation of faithful followership and add to it with your own insights.

1

Welcome to ~~Leadership~~ Followership

ARE YOU CALLED TO be a leader? By the number of leadership books, podcasts, and even doctoral programs available, it would seem that nearly everyone is called to be a leader—or at least wishes so. As important as all of these calls to leadership are, there's a foundational aspect that we must not forget. *Followership*. For as we go about our life journeys, with some reaching leadership position, it is important that we follow well all along the way, learning what it means to be an excellent follower. Thus, this book is for all—those just beginning or well into their working years, those yearning for leadership while stuck underneath an unwelcomed ceiling in church or marriage, those shunning leadership roles as well as those who lead.

Unlike leadership, the number of books on followership is modest—even miniscule. Moreover, many of them address followership in the context of leadership with titles like *Followership: A Practical Guide to Aligning Leaders and Followers* or *The Art of Followership: How Great Followers Create Great Leaders and Organizations.* Notice how it's difficult to discuss followership without talking about leadership; the following chapters will often do the same. Further, as the field of organizational studies has begun to

Followership

address followership by focusing on *courageous followership*, Coggins provides three models of courageous followership which we will take up in chapter five.[1]

While this new area of study is helpful, the effort relates mainly to the workplace; moreover, while typologies are helpful, there is much territory to cover well beyond the workplace. Thus, the goal of this chapter—and the entire book—is to broaden our focus.

Everyone—at each step of the way—needs to follow well. No matter where we are in life, we follow the lead of others. When I was a college president—truly a leadership role—I had to follow the lead of the board of trustees as they held high the mission of the college before all of us. When I was a denominational chief executive, I had to follow the lead of a Board of Trustees who represented the thousands of people who had found a home in that denomination. I can't think of one role where a leader doesn't have to follow a board, a mission statement, those who elected him or her, or some other group or document. Leaders who seemingly have no accountability, however, are those of whom we must be wary.

So, as we begin, we first need to look at the individual and his or her personality characteristics. Thankfully, there are a great number of ways to assess one's personality characteristics. I like to use CliftonStrengths by Gallup. The results can help one see his or her personal characteristics more clearly. Not so many years ago, Leigh Buchanan compared the characteristics of a sample of the CEOs of Fortune 500 companies and a nationwide sample of entrepreneurs using a specially developed form of the CliftonStrengths.[2] In examining ten areas, the CEOs scored higher in each case than the entrepreneurs. These ten areas included *risk-taker, business focus, determination, delegator, knowledge-seeker, creative thinker, confidence, promoter, independence,* and *relationship builder.*

Of course, this kind of study can be criticized, since most CEOs are white males—gender or cultural differences won't show up in the results. In addition, since similar studies are not available for non-entrepreneurs (in this case, followers), it is worth our while

---

1. Coggins, "Three Models," para. 1.
2. Buchanan, "Inside the Mind of the Entrepreneur," para. 16.

Welcome to ~~Leadership~~ Followership

to ask which of these characteristics are important for those of us who follow. I sent out a query to my fourteen hundred-plus Facebook friends, asking them to identify from among these characteristics which two or three are important for following well. Being a *relationship builder* and a *knowledge-seeker* zoomed to the top. Following after the first two were *determination* and *creative thinker*.

Let's think about each of these. If I'm asked to follow a leader in the workplace, it is almost never the case that following is a solo affair. I recall one summer job during college where I tried my best to follow the directives of the manager, only to be thwarted by co-workers who were uninterested in following and even resorted to sabotage to avoid work. Sadly, as a college student, I was unable to build relationships with these co-workers—and soon the summer was over. But if this would have been my life calling, I would have had to build relationships—one at a time—that would reflect trust and eventually to following well as a team.

Seeking knowledge while following is also critical to success. Especially in the workplace, training welcomes the new employee in orientation. Some places have continuing education all along the way. Thus, acquiring knowledge is important in following well—following the boss's instructions—that sometimes means picking up the nuances and the unspoken cues, following the protocols in the warehouse that have been developed for reasons of safety and efficiency, following the patterns of pacing and productivity in work which are often learned by not only listening to those who you follow, but watching closely as well. Yet, the need is not just *acquiring* knowledge; it's *seeking* knowledge. No matter the context or the number of levels of which to be aware in following, passive and inactive followers learn little. But those who are engaged, ask questions, and figure things out are the champions of followership; moreover, it stands to reason that a knowledge-seeker is better equipped for the discernment needed in followership. (Notice, too, that when we review the three models of courageous followership, the best followers are those who think critically, asking important questions.)

Followership

At first, I was surprised to see being a creative thinker was selected often by my Facebook friends, but upon further reflection, it ties into the previous paragraph, this sentence in particular: *But those who are engaged, ask questions, and figure things out are the champions of followership.* Indeed, figuring things out takes creativity. Followership should not be done with robot-like automation. Such non-thinking could lead to disastrous results at worst and dullness at best. Much better is to follow with creativity, inserting your own insights and reflections into your followership. The result will be better engagement and even joy.

Finally, determination. While it seems to be the case that entrepreneurial leaders need determination, I believe those of us who follow do as well. We can look at this in two ways. Unlike the leader whose determination is rewarded often with high pay and attractive perks, those of us who follow often do not have immediate rewards for our stick-to-itiveness. We might be noticed for our diligence but more often we are not. We might be rewarded for sticking to a project with the utmost of determination, but that is the exceptional situation. Instead, diligence is simply expected, rarely noticed and even more seldomly rewarded. Nevertheless, the determination exhibited by those who follow reflect personal characteristics and values that feed, at least, personal satisfaction.

Now let's dive below the characteristic that leaders and followers display and into something deeper in the personality—ego strength.

The concept of the ego arises from psychoanalytic theory, and according to the American Psychological Association's definition, ego strength is,

> in psychoanalytic theory, the ability of the ego to maintain an effective balance between the inner impulses of the id, the superego, and outer reality. An individual with a strong ego is thus one who is able to tolerate frustration and stress, postpone gratification, modify selfish desires when necessary, and resolve internal conflicts and emotional problems before they lead to neurosis.[3]

3. "Ego Strength"

Welcome to ~~Leadership~~ Followership

But one doesn't need to be a student of psychoanalytic theory to understand ego-strength, for the term has developed meaning well beyond its psychoanalytic roots. The term is used by many and at its core relates to the strength (or weakness) a person finds in the sense of self.

I maintain that leaders typically exhibit robust ego-strength. In the research we reviewed from CEOs and entrepreneurs, traits like *confidence* and *independence* and even *risk-taker* demonstrate the bedrock set of characteristics for CEOs and especially for those who are entrepreneurs. But I also maintain that followers need to develop ego-strength as well. For just as leaders need confidence and independence, so do those of us who follow. Being a follower doesn't mean someone always holds your hand. It means that when you follow, you often have to step out with certainty and confidence, with self-assuredness and self-worth.

I recall that my first months and beyond in the role of college president required me to boost my own sense of confidence. I noticed that people wanted direction and even answers, not my musings and reflections. I remember when I spoke in front of groups, I not only needed something important to say, but I also needed to speak well. I recall a colleague recognizing my need, and drilling me to follow the old adage of telling the audience what you're going to say, saying it, and then telling them what you've said.

But it's just not leaders who need this kind of confidence and strength. When I directed student academic services in the college setting, I was required to participate in the admissions committee—the group that made decisions about whether to admit or reject applicants whose profiles were on the border. After a year of being frustrated with relying on gut feelings, I ran some correlation studies between entering ACT scores (as well as other variables) and retention, suggesting to the team that these were data we could rely upon. I was the newcomer and rather young, but ego-strength was required to creatively follow while making suggestions to my older peers that fit within and even improved the implementation of college policies. Then, when I was a dean for instruction, I followed the lead of a wonderful provost who gave me great responsibilities with little direction. As the need for assessment was entering higher education at the end of the last century, the provost trusted me to figure out not only how to work with academic departments on developing their assessment plans, but also how to use approaches that allowed individuality yet similarity among the various departments. From mathematics to classics, I needed to interact with colleagues who often had little interest in or use for outcome assessments. In short, I needed ego-strength.

However, for leaders and followers alike, when that ego-strength begins to crowd out concern for others, we call it *egocentrism*.

"I know, I know, egocentric." That's a statement our adult son with Down syndrome has used over and over. Why? Because when he thinks just about himself, forgetting others, we cue him and say, "Paul, what are we going to say?"

Great leaders are those who have learned to avoid egocentrism and its nearly exclusive focus on self and instead focus on the needs of others. We see examples all around us of these two types. All who ascend to the presidency of the United States have a sturdy degree of ego-strength; stated differently, all have a strong sense of self. Those who have erred have failed to avoid having that strength slide into ego-centrism. One former president thought he could take advantage of an intern; another spoke with aggressive words with little regard for how some would act upon those words. Those who have succeeded have kept their egocentrism at bay, working with others to lead well.

The same is true for great followers. We who follow know those we want to work with and those we wish to avoid—those with nearly exclusive focus on themselves. Some of our fellow followers are wannabes. They want to be the leader and believe even in the trenches that they must assert themselves in ways that have their egos crowding out others.

Then, of course, there are those who don't seek the presidency or leadership positions available to them. While they may have incredible ego-strength, they are at home with their sense of self (often selfless people) and their calling irrespective of the degree of leadership required. Moreover, they are nearly void of egocentrism or they excel at pushing back on egocentric tendencies.

But back to the main point. All are called to followership. Those who are egocentric or selfless, those who possess balanced ego-strength, whether driven to leadership or not. And while gender and culture may also influence *how* we follow (addressed in successive chapters), all are called to followership.

Core to my worldview is God's word, the Bible. It is here where the call to follow is rooted in God's sovereignty and his creation: humanity. If we turn to the first chapter of the book of Genesis, verse 28, we read that after creating Adam and Eve, God gave them instructions that they were to follow:

> God blessed them and said to them, "Be fruitful and increase in number; fill the earth and subdue it. Rule over the fish in the sea and the birds in the sky and over every living creature that moves on the ground."

Then, in the next chapter we read another instruction: Not to eat of the tree of the knowledge of good and evil. In this history of our first father and mother, God makes sure they know *who* and *what* to follow: to be followers of God and to succeed at stewardship. Yet they failed this first test of following and the result has tainted all of humanity.

But then, we should zoom ahead to the New Testament, where God sacrificially provides his Son for our salvation. There we read dozens of times where Jesus says "follow me," showing a new way by which followership is required of us. Jesus said "follow me" to gather together his band of disciples; many times, he also added what the cost of following would be. Luke 9:23 says "Then he said to them all: 'Whoever wants to be my disciple must deny themselves and take up their cross daily and follow me.'" Mark 10:21 states this: "Jesus looked at him and loved him. 'One thing you lack,' he said. 'Go, sell everything you have and give to the poor, and you will have treasure in heaven. Then come, follow me.'" Echoes are found elsewhere in Matt 19:21, Mark 8:34, and Luke 18:22, for example.

Followership

Not only does Jesus call us to follow him; we learn about followership as Jesus followed the will of his Father. In the garden of Gethsemane, right before his crucifixion, Jesus wrestled with what lay ahead. His first words, recorded in Matt 26:39b, are "My Father, if it is possible, may this cup be taken from me. Yet not as I will, but as you will." In his next prayer in verse 42, he voices the same sentiment: "My Father, if it is not possible for this cup to be taken away unless I drink it, may your will be done." The third time, in verse 44, Scripture says only this: "so he left them and went away once more and prayed the third time, saying the same thing."

Note, too, the contrast going on while Jesus wrestles. While he reflects perfect submission in the face of fear (showing both his divine and human nature) his three disciples can't follow a simple instruction to stay awake and wait.

So what have we learned about followership? It is required of all, as shown in the Bible and necessary for all of life. Also, those who lead may have a set of characteristics built upon strong egos, but some of those very same characteristics are needed in following well. In addition, we've learned that we all need to keep our egocentrism in-check and be focused on others whether called to followership or uniquely called to leadership.

Will we be perfect followers? We not only have the garden of Gethsemane events from which to learn, but we should listen as well to the interchange the Gospel of Mark gives us in chapter 12:29–31 as Jesus asks us to be focused on God and neighbor:

> "The most important one," answered Jesus, "is this: 'Hear, O Israel: The LORD our God, the LORD is one. Love the LORD your God with all your heart and with all your soul and with all your mind and with all your strength.' The second is this: 'Love your neighbor as yourself.' There is no commandment greater than these."

Certainly, this focus is a needed and powerful check to egocentrism. Our problem of course, is that what we know isn't how we act. Notice the response of the questioner in chapter 12:32–34, followed by Jesus' reply:

Welcome to ~~Leadership~~ Followership

"Well said, teacher," the man replied. "You are right in saying that God is one and there is no other but him. To love him with all your heart, with all your understanding and with all your strength, and to love your neighbor as yourself is more important than all burnt offerings and sacrifices." When Jesus saw that he had answered wisely, he said to him, "You are not far from the kingdom of God."

"Not far from the kingdom of God." What does that mean? First, Jesus could be noting that until love of self is replaced by a wholehearted love of God, a person isn't saved. In other words, on the verge of committing one's life to Christ, but not yet having fully surrendered. This interpretation suggests that when using the term *kingdom of God*, Jesus is focusing on whether someone is now and for eternity receiving membership in God's kingdom. This interpretation fits nicely with other teachings of Jesus. Matt 19:23-24 records Jesus saying this:

> Then Jesus said to his disciples, "Truly I tell you, it is hard for someone who is rich to enter the kingdom of heaven. Again I tell you, it is easier for a camel to go through the eye of a needle than for someone who is rich to enter the kingdom of God."

Jesus is responding to a questioner who asked how to obtain *eternal life*. So notice, Jesus uses the same term as the passage from Mark 12, *kingdom of God*, to denote salvation in him for eternity.

While this first interpretation has eternal value, there is a second interpretation that is more dynamic. We need to back up a bit to understand this interpretation.

I grew up in a faith tradition that used a rich yet simple phrase to understand the times in which we live: *The kingdom of God—now and yet coming*. It's a wonderful phrase. Jesus came and so we live in the reality of the kingdom he brought with him, moving Old Testament people from a theocracy into a community. But that community is not yet fully established. So, at times we long for Jesus' return—the full establishment of God's kingdom, especially when the dark clouds gather and our lives lose hope.

Followership

Yet it's important to remember that Jesus has already come. During his earthly sojourn, he ushered in the kingdom of God. True, we await his return for the complete fulfillment of that kingdom life, but we have ample evidence of what life in the kingdom of God should mean—now!

In the passages we just looked at, we see two of many descriptions of how kingdom life should work *now*. Loving neighbor as self! What a radical way of living. It means giving up possessions to benefit those in need, thinking more of others than self, and a whole lot more. The Gospels are full of descriptions. The beatitudes provide an amazing list of qualities; each parable gives us a lesson for living life now.

The beauty of the phrase *now and yet coming* shows us life as a process. *Sanctification* is an old term with great meaning—the process of becoming sanctified or holy. When one turns one's life over to Christ with total love, it doesn't mean that we are changed instantaneously. No, it's a journey, a process of becoming more and more holy. Our love of self—our egocentrism—doesn't immediately disappear, but it should become less and less central to our thoughts and actions as our focus on God first and then neighbor takes over.

So when Jesus says the questioner is not far from the kingdom of God, it may be that Jesus is telling us loving God is a journey—moving toward God. Coupled with our first interpretation, we are all on a journey. True, there is a necessary point when we consciously seek to abandon our love of self and direct our love to God. But before then and after then, we are on a journey. For those of us who have accepted membership in the new kingdom, we still struggle with self-interest, possession accumulation, and forgetting our neighbors nearby and far away. But when loving God is central, little by little we lose those old attractions and become more and more focused on our love for God. We become faithful followers.

In the ensuing chapters we will look more closely at what is required to be faithful followers in a number of dimensions—looking at followership during the transition into adulthood, implications for gender and culture, and then understanding followership

Welcome to ~~Leadership~~ Followership

in marriage and family, in church and the Christian community, in the workplace, and in society.

Concluding Reflections

As I reflect upon my college presidency days, as a leader I had to follow well in a number of ways. First and most important was to listen.

Alumni and donors expected that their opinions counted and I would seek to follow their suggestions, using the gift of discernment, separating the diamonds from the rock as well as exercising truthfulness in response. I recall one friend of the college who pressed for adding an aeronautics program—something quite distant from our collection of majors and minors. I pointed out the difficulties but didn't say no. In the end, it was a non-starter but yet a creative idea and I valued him because of his willingness to think outside the box. Another friend of the college suggested we add a vice president to oversee existing facilities as well as lead the efforts at expanding the campus with new buildings. I listened and soon we hired for that position; George came on board and became an indispensable part of the leadership team and a wise friend and colleague as well.

Listening to faculty was also essential, following their suggestions—again with discernment. All universities have elaborate faculty governance structures in place so that faculty committees channel their voice in a way that makes participation with the administration possible. Of course, some administrative leaders block such input and participation, and stalemates can lead to votes of no confidence or worse. I remember, however, some of the best ideas arising from such a shared structure. As we stepped into graduate programs, the faculty led with program design and pedagogy; we as administrators needed to listen so as to market and admit students into these new programs.

Best of all was listening to students and following their lead. During the Obama administration, the White House Office of Faith-Based and Neighborhood Partnerships offered a program

Followership

to universities: The President's Interfaith and Community Service Campus Challenge. Notice the two key terms: *interfaith* and *community service*. I immediately became interested in the possibility that we would join this effort: what better place to prepare for an interfaith world than on university campuses in the context of their communities? However, rather than asking a faculty committee whether we should participate in the program, I asked the students, going to the student body president. The response was an enthusiastic "Yes!"

Because there was a large Arab-American community in our vicinity, we sought the advice of a local Muslim leader which required listening to how he thought we could pull this off in partnership. Together we focused on the installation of a walking trail along a waterway in our community. And the students from Trinity Christian College and local Muslim students attending a range of universities stepped up!

An interesting side note about this project bears mentioning. Had I gone the faculty route for approval, I'm certain I would have encountered a bit of fear along the way: "Would our students be swayed by the Muslim students they would be working alongside?" While I was convinced our students needed preparation for an interfaith world, and I suspected it would be a positive growing experience for them, the latter was just a hypothesis. So, taking a more empirical approach, I revised a survey tool found in the faith formation literature and used it before and after the project with both sets of students. As I suspected, the experience for the Trinity Christian College students strengthened their own Christian faith, although we didn't see the same faith strengthening among the Muslim students.

And finally, while my shared leadership with the Trinity Christian College students in this project was exhilarating, I may have failed as a leader when I kept this project mostly out of the college's public news channels. I feared too many readers would think the worst of such interfaith efforts and I was content to let the experience be contained to the growth and friendships the two sets of students experienced. In other words, in the process

Welcome to ~~Leadership~~ Followership

of discernment, I chose to follow the lead of students and partner with local Muslim leaders, relying less on faculty engagement and avoiding more public feedback rooted in fear or racism.

2

Following the Leader

The Role of Gender

By the number of leadership books, podcasts, and seminars, it seems we are all motivated to step into leadership. I don't believe it needs to be so. Take my wife for example. She has wrapped up nearly four decades as a nurse educator. First at Calvin University, then at Trinity Christian College, and then again at Calvin University, she has steadily refused to step onto the path of departmental leadership. She knows her sweet spot—teaching nursing students—and has sought no other leadership role in higher education. Same thing at church. She has been an elder, but has shied away from most leadership roles. She once served as a co-chair of a nonprofit board, and couldn't wait for that term to end!

The question of this chapter is whether there are differences rooted in gender that influence following well. To address this question we need to look at leadership as well. Consider what the *Harvard Business Review* has to say:

> Highly intelligent, confident, and successful, alpha males represent about 70% of all senior executives. As the label implies, they're the people who aren't happy unless they're the top dogs—the ones calling the shots. Although there are plenty of successful female leaders with

Following the Leader—The Role of Gender

equally strong personalities, we've found top women rarely if ever match the complete alpha profile.... Alphas reach the top ranks in large organizations because they are natural leaders—comfortable with responsibility in a way non-alphas can never be. Most people feel stress when they have to make important decisions; alphas get stressed when tough decisions don't rest in their capable hands. For them, being in charge delivers such a thrill, they willingly take on levels of responsibility most rational people would find overwhelming.[1]

However, zeroing in on alpha males does not provide complete understanding. In the previous chapter, we discussed ego-strength and the dangers of leading to egocentrism—thinking about the self well before others. Another dimension of this discussion is *narcissism*. A meta-review of the literature, spanning nearly twenty five years and including 355 studies, was completed by Emily Grijalva and colleagues. The first task of this group of researchers was to reflect on narcissism: "Narcissism is associated with various interpersonal dysfunctions, including the general inability to maintain healthy long-term relationships . . . and unethical and/or exploitative behaviors . . . At the same time, narcissism has a seemingly positive relationship with some indicators of psychological health such as self-esteem and emotional stability, and evidence suggests that narcissists tend to emerge as leaders."[2] For while we all enjoy the role of armchair psychologist, pointing out when someone is narcissistic, we need to remember that narcissistic characteristics can have some positive outcomes (including assuming leadership roles), but full narcissism results in dysfunction on the part of the individual.

Their meta-review found that men and women differ in their degree of narcissism. Many of the reports they reviewed related to the NPI (Narcissistic Personality Inventory), a well-accepted tool for assessing narcissism.

---

1. Ludeman and Erlandson, "Coaching the Alpha Male," para. 1.
2. Grijalva et al., "Gender Differences in Narcissism," 262.

Followership

> We found the largest gender difference for the E/E facet [the Exploitative/Entitlement facet of the NPI]. This result suggests that compared with women, men are more likely to exploit others and to believe that they themselves are special and therefore entitled to privileges. The second largest gender difference (also favoring men) was for the L/A [Leadership/Authority] facet of narcissism. In other words, compared with women men exhibit more assertiveness, motivation to lead, and a desire for power and authority over others.

Before concluding that this difference in gender abounds as men and women journey together, the authors provide this important observation:

> We must therefore emphasize that the gender differences referred to in this article do not apply to every individual within a group. Not all men are entitled or exploitative. Not all women are low in a sense of leadership and motivation for authority. The current results are consistent with the finding that within-group trait differences are generally larger than differences between gender groups (Hyde, 2005). Although we are saying that the average man tends to be more narcissistic than the average woman, we are not making generalizations to specific individuals. In fact, the current results might be seen as consistent with the gender similarities hypothesis, or the idea that women and men are often more similar than different when it comes to many psychological attributes.[3]

With this understanding, a study by Italian researchers, Rovelli and Curnis,[4] provides a compelling review of how narcissism in men drives them toward leadership. They found that those with higher degrees of narcissism (measured by the NPI) moved 29% faster in their careers to the CEO position than those without a narcissistic profile. They cite other studies that have demonstrated the harm a narcissistic leader can do to organizations (installing an individualistic culture in the organization, reducing collaborating

---

3. Grijalva et al., "Gender Differences in Narcissism," 283.
4. Rovelli and Curnis, "Perks of Narcissism," para. 37.

and integrity, making rash and risky decisions) and, of course, the results can be exceedingly troublesome for those who are compelled to follow the leader.

I've witnessed firsthand the ascents of narcissists and the trouble they cause. If you are following a narcissist's lead, each day becomes a challenge. While there's no survival manual for those following a narcissist whose motives are causing harm, I'd invite you to focus on values. When compromise is no longer an option, sometimes walking away is appropriate.

The pandemic that began in 2020 may have given witness to walking away. The "great resignation" was a time when many walked away from jobs and positions. For some, the pandemic gave them time to reflect and realign their values, causing them to depart their current positions. While I'm not suggesting those who walked did so because they had a narcissistic boss, reports suggested that oftentimes departures related to conflicting values as people asked deep, purpose-of-life questions.

The storming of the US Capitol Building in January of 2021 evidenced many walking into conflict, but one trial in particular demonstrated a poignant decision to walk away from a parent whose narcissism turned into paranoia. Jackson Reffitt saw the warning signs in his father, Guy Reffitt, and took bold action, ending up on the witness stand.

> Well, at the start of the testimony, his dad burst into tears. His mom was in the gallery, also quite emotional. Jackson was soft-spoken, calm. He's not been in close touch with his family since turning his dad in to the FBI, and he waved at his mom as he left the court.[5]

Back to gender. So what do we make of gender differences in leadership? As Grijalva and colleagues concluded that on average men tend to be more narcissistic, we can't assume anything specific to individuals. We also know that at least in the world of work, narcissistic men advance more rapidly to the leadership positions;

---

5. Martinez and Dreisbach, "Son Takes the Stand."

further, the leadership of males in church and in family is often a given by some according to their scriptural interpretation.

What's even more interesting, however, is to speculate what this means for followership. It means that on average, narcissism is less pronounced in women, and women are often not the leaders in the workplace, in many churches, and even in some families. Does this mean women are better followers or that they just wear their leadership roles in less attention-commanding ways?

It is helpful to look at this question historically. Reading Kristen Kobes Du Mez's book, *Jesus and John Wayne*,[6] I was reminded of the seventies—a time during which I entered and graduated from college, met and married my wife, and began to develop lifelong patterns. Du Mez cites Marabel Morgan's book *The Total Woman* as being significant during this era for evangelicals. Using the lens of followership, it seems Morgan's approach was to assume male headship, and in following the lead of her husband, the wife was to excel in strengthening her husband's ego by offering great meals and even greater sex. In other words, followership for women meant complete devotion to men.

That approach didn't go over well in our relationship as we were dating, then engaged, and finally married. We choose wedding vows that mirrored the other's, pledging that each of us would develop God's gifts in the other—not having one as the traditional breadwinner and the other greeting her spouse wrapped in Saran wrap (which Du Mez points out was never included in Morgan's book).

While a subsequent chapter brings us more fully into the topic of marriage, it is helpful to more directly address gender roles in followership. Consider this hypothesis: As a group, women may be less narcissistic than men; therefore, as a group, women may more readily take up the task of followership.

Notice a few things. First, the term *as a group* is used. In other words, each individual may or may not follow the group pattern.

Second, I suspect this pattern is fluid, as socialization continues to change for girls and women. While there are still glass

---

6. DuMez, *Jesus and John Wayne*.

Following the Leader—The Role of Gender

ceilings for women, many women are willing and eager to break through them.

Third, narcissism or the lack thereof is not the only important dimension of leadership or followership. Consider characteristics we've already addressed: *determination, knowledge-seeker, relationship builder.* Are there gender differences in these qualities?

Gino and Brooks unpack determination and ambition in the context of striving for success:

> Being ambitious means having or showing a strong desire and determination to succeed. But success, especially professional success, means different things to different people. To some, professional success means achieving power over others and making a lot of money. To others, it means being happy at work, making other people happy, or helping others. And for most people, it probably includes a combination of these outcomes with differing weights of importance. So, if one defines professional ambition narrowly as achieving power over others, then women are less ambitious. But most people—especially women—do not define professional success in this narrow way. It is possible that men and women are correctly predicting the differential experiences that they would encounter with professional advancement and are making sound decisions. It is also possible that women are overestimating the negative consequences associated with power, that men are underestimating them, or both. We can conclude, however, that one reason women may not assume high-level positions in organizations is that they believe, unlike men, that doing so would require them to compromise other important life goals.[7]

What might some of those important life goals include? One of the first that comes to mind is the desire to have children—where the role of the woman begins with pregnancy—an experience significantly different from that of the man. Tennis great Serena Williams retired from tennis for child-bearing but complained the

---

7. Gino and Brooks, "Explaining Gender Differences" paras. 15–17.

Followership

gender difference was not fair.[8] But back to our main question: does this ability to project consequences while holding multiple life goals relate to followership?

A dimension of this question relates to the breadth of vision. For the sake of this discussion, let's assume there is a continuum from 360 vision (the ability to see the interplay of social and personal dimensions at present and project them into the future) to narcissistic vision (the ability to only see the current context and future implications in light of the impact on oneself). We may assume, from what we've already reviewed that, as a group, women are closer to the 360 vision end of the continuum and men, as a group, to the narcissistic vision end.

With this continuum in mind, we may be able to presume that women may be better at understanding followership. Notice the word *understanding*. That doesn't mean women are better at followership; my hypothesis is only that women can read the situations involving followership better. The correct term for this is social cognition: "cognition in which people perceive, think about, interpret, categorize, and judge their own social behaviors and those of others."[9] In general, study after study demonstrates that women have higher levels of specific components of social cognition than men. It stands to reason, then, that women as a group are better at understanding social situations—a key component of following well. For followership requires not only understanding oneself, but also those leading.

Does that mean, then, that women are better at following than men? Understanding a social relationship or situation—current or projected for the future—does not necessarily translate into better or more helpful behavior, although it provides a necessary advantage. As I've observed followership in men and women, anecdotally I've noticed that some men can be more error-prone—misreading the social situation out of profound egocentricism. The know-it-all male quickly comes to mind. Perhaps the lack of such

---

8. Hanson, "Serena Williams Says She Had to Choose," paras. 1–3.
9. "Social Cognition."

behavior among women, as a group, indicates that their stronger ability to read social situations allows them to follow better.

This literature can also give us insight into gender differences and relationship building. If women, as a group, may have greater social cognitive skills in reading others and situations, they may have the foundational skills needed for buildling relationships. Further, as studies show, women tend to be more relationally-oriented than men. In his review of relationship styles of men and women, Gregg Henriques refers to Carol Gilligan's book *In a Different Voice* that focuses on women as more relational than men in moral reasoning and the work of Alice Eagly, who explains gender roles with men being more agentic and women being more communal.[10]

Again, back to our question: does this mean women are better suited for followership than men? The answer has to be both "yes" and "no." Yes, because following is all about the relationship—from building the relationship to maintaining the relationship between leader and follower as well as relationships among the followers. But with relational strengths comes the risk for overvaluing and overrelying on relationships—thereby introducing potential conflict and hurt. Sometimes the agentic nature of men may be more helpful in maintaining relationships between leaders and followers. An agentic state "occurs when individuals, as subordinates to a higher authority in an organized status hierarchy, feel compelled to obey the orders issued by that authority."[11]

While I need to be careful of stereotypes, I have witnessed over the years college departments that are all male and those that are all female. While sometimes all male departments seem to need more relational capacity and all female departments need to rely less on relationships, the best academic department in my experience has been those comprised of both men and women.

Finally, we must examine the characteristic of knowledge seeking as it relates to gender and followership. A probing study by Cristina Poleacovschi and colleagues looked at knowledge accessibility—the time and effort spent in seeking knowledge—in the

10. Henriques, "Relationship Styles," para. 7.
11. "Agentic State."

workership.[12] They found that in general, women perceived higher levels of knowledge accessibility than men, and it was the highest when seeking knowledge from other women. Not surprising, the lowest perceived accessibility was when men's search for knowledge required seeking that knowledge from women.

Might this study mean that knowledge-seeking—a characteristic important in following well—might be stronger among women (especially woman-to-woman) than men? Indeed, it may be the case that, as a group, women's desire for seeking knowledge puts them in a better position for following well—including that seeking knowledge may better equip them for the discernment needed in followership.

What have we concluded? As a group, women may exhibit some of the characteristics that provide them an advantage in followership. However, we remain compromised, as we still live with the vestiges of women's socialization that required them to play second fiddle. If we notice women who follow well, is it because of superior skills and appropriate personal characteristics, or is it because of repressive socialization? Rather than presuming we can find an answer in such a situation, we have new generations of women whose socialization has differed radically from that of their mothers and grandmothers, providing great encouragement for women in leadership and followership. I'm excited as I anticipate the pathways my four daughters and three granddaughters will take in life.

Concluding Reflections

After looking at research on gender differences and speculating upon its relationship to followership, it's helpful to reflect anecdotally on life experiences. This chapter began with my observation that my wife's desire has not been leadership. In many ways, however, the observations of this chapter can be seen in her academic career.

12. Poleacovschi et al., "Gendered Knowledge," 1–10.

Following the Leader—The Role of Gender

One of the clearest gender differences I've noted over the years is her involvement in the role of research. While research goals and activities among those pursuing the academic calling can be very competitive, I've noticed that in her career and in the department of nursing where she taught, research was often more collaborative in nature. Joining together in a research project provided opportunity for building and strengthening relationships among faculty members, not for the erecting of competitive barriers. Indeed, her department was comprised mostly of women, and I think this quality produced a unique opportunity for shared scholarship.

A second observation I've noticed in my wife's career and her desire to mostly avoid leadership roles has related to her ability, at any given point in time, to look at a wider array of life goals without having one obscure any others. Before we had children and were both at the University of Michigan, I sought and obtained a PhD; she sought and obtained an MS. Did that mean she was less determined? No. She saw life in a more complete dimension: that children would be a very real and demanding stage of life. She eventually entered a PhD program when our youngest of four biological children was in kindergarten. Was she limited in ambition and determination? No, she simply saw all of the puzzle pieces and recognized a different way of proceeding than my more simplistic way.

So, is my wife better at followership? A number of answers come to mind.

First, she has always been content with her own identity. While these qualities have led to little interest in leadership roles, this hasn't meant she has been a blind follower all these years. Instead, she has taken up life with a healthy sense of independence. While she was the "first lady" when I was president of Trinity Christian College, she was also a nursing faculty member. While she served well in the first lady role, her professional identity rested in her nursing faculty role. Moreover, I think she modeled especially for women students that one's professional identity needn't be limited to its link to a partner's position. Thus, while she followed participation expectations that many had for a president's spouse (to attend countless

Followership

dinners, events, and activities), she did so in a way that added value to any occasion—value springing from her role of faculty member, a mother, and, yes, the wife of the college president.

Second, knowledge-seeking. In our marriage, I've always been the one quick to make decisions—important decisions. Barb has been the one who has sought added time and information before coming to a decision. The most dramatic example was when we adopted three Ethiopian siblings when we were in our early fifties.

Our lifelong friends had met these children when they were initially orphaned, even helping them furnish a small little twenty foot by twenty foot house for them, separate from but under the supervision of an orphanage. When the oldest boy of this family reminded our friends six years later that they were still parentless, our friends asked us and others if we had an interest in adoption.

True to form, I immediately wished to pursue the adoption. Barb pondered the idea for a few weeks, asked important questions, and then concluded that we shouldn't pursue this opportunity. Rather than relying on emotions alone (as was my response), she sought to understand the requirements, challenges, and long-term implications. Yet, that next Sunday we listened to a sermon on Jesus commanding Peter to get out of the boat. While Barb wasn't aiming to walk on water, she recognized this most significant charge was the truth she needed to hear before saying yes to the adoption.

Indeed, we all need to follow well—most certainly on what God requires of us. Whether it's a difference in gender or simply in personal characteristics, Barb has always recognized the chief requirement of followship is discernment—discernment that is faith-filled and faithful.

3

Following the Leader

The Role of Culture and Race

WHEN WE LIVED ADJACENT to the Navajo reservation, I had to re-learn body language. Looking down—not into one's eyes—was actually a sign of respect, not disrespect. In conversations, I would usually put my hands in my pocket to silently cue myself to slow down, listen, and refrain from interjecting. When we adopted an Ethiopian sibling group, I had to learn that spoken agreement can mean "yes, I hear you" instead of "yes, I will," for the former is required to show respect to an elder. Might there be something culturally-based about whether there is a quest for leadership? And what does that mean for followership?

The question is not *if,* but *how* culture plays a difference. Culture may *wrap* the quest for the exercise of leadership in differing ways. For example, Navajo leaders may embed their goals and actions with a drive toward harmony, a chief value of Navajo culture. Of course, the examples are as many as there are cultural groups. Many have studied this impact, and cultural differences on a global scale can be stark:

> Leaders are expected to have vision, but how this is displayed differs from culture to culture. In China, the influence of Confucian values makes people wary of leaders

Followership

who talk without engaging in specific action. Indian managers, on the other hand, care less about visionaries, preferring bold assertive styles of leadership. Communication skills are also important to the leader, but again, how these skills are perceived differs among and within cultures. What constitutes a good communicator is likely to vary greatly across cultures. American managers are more likely to provide directions to subordinates on a face-to-face basis while Japanese managers are likely to use written memos. In the U.S. subordinates are usually provided negative feedback directly from their supervisors, while in Japan such feedback is usually channeled through a peer of the subordinates. These differences reflect the U.S. individualistic norm of "brute honesty" and the Japanese collectivistic norm of "face-saving."[1]

My wife and I have learned in our mixed cultural family (four adult biological children with one whose spouse is Ethiopian while the other two spouses are of European descent; three adult Ethiopian children with one married to a fellow Ethiopian and the other to a Liberian) that leading and following is curious at times. A family dinner gathering, for example, often results in some of our adult children arriving on time and others late (notice my cultural bias in using terms like *on time* and *late*). Our family, thankfully, has provided ongoing learning opportunities, with my wife and I always learning how to follow culturally determined norms. If you can call the parents of adult children "leaders" (some would argue they no longer lead their offspring), we have learned to follow the lead of our adult children, recognizing culture shapes each of them and we have to "give up" one aspect of our leading. Going back to the example of gathering them all together for a meal, we have learned that it isn't productive to focus on our culturally embedded sense of *on time* and *late,* but rather simply experience the meal time to be a time of coming and going. In other words, when putting together those of more than one culture, it is incredibly important to follow the cultural lead of each individual rather than presuming one culture must be dominant and correct.

1. Knowledge at Wharton Staff, "Cultural Factors," para. 7.

Following the Leader—The Role of Culture and Race

Earlier I mentioned our Ethiopian children using "yes" to indicate they have heard, but one should not assume they necessarily agree. In many ways, this is a positive way to follow a leader, if the leader understands the true meaning. For "yes" means "I've heard you and I give you my respect." Of course, the leader needs to be attentive to situations when the follower has said "yes" but does not follow; then, the task is to discern what is going on: a difference of opinion, a delay in initiation, or following in a way that is more inclusive and not relying just on the specific leader at a specific point in time.

Indeed, one of the biggest disruptions between followers and leaders may often be the result of differing cultural backgrounds and expectations. When Barack Obama was president of the US, there were those who were unable to follow or appreciate his leadership simply based on his Kenyan roots and related skin tone; some, like authors Richard Fording and Sanford Schram, believe his presidency was one of the factors giving rise to white nationalism.[2]

When I was a college president and Obama was elected, there was a rise in racist responses. When student perpetrators could be identified, student discipline resulted, such as the case with displaying the Confederate flag. When no perpetuator could be found, such as with the posting of a racial slur on the doors to the chapel, I personally removed the posting before 7:00 a.m. so as to avoid the hurt that was intended and the attention that was sought by the anonymous perpetuator.

Why is it so difficult to follow the lead of someone whose culture or race differs from one's own? We all know the sin of racism, brought on by individuals as well as systems and the conscious or subconscious desire to maintain white privilege. I've been in a work situation where the white "followers" diminished, by means of delay and other passive-aggressive means, the authority of the leader who was African-American and a woman. Especially among white males, it is troubling to recognize that there can be this reaction against following a leader of a different culture or race. Why might this be?

2. Fording and Schram, *Hard White*.

Followership

Earlier we learned that ego strength is the ability "to tolerate frustration and stress, postpone gratification, modify selfish desires when necessary, and resolve internal conflicts and emotional problems." Certainly, if being a follower of a leader whose culture or race differs from one's own is problematic, then ego strength is not sufficiently developed. And a unique and twisted form of egocentrism results: the belief that me and only those like me are important and capable. In such cases it doesn't take much study to understand that often some with little education, few resources, and impoverished experiences can quickly fall into this trap of rejecting a leader from a different culture or racial background. Moreover, then the second trap arises: the desire to follow someone who appeals to their ego-centrism—often forming connections on race (white), gender (male), and power (fear of losing power).

I believe the high school and college years are critical for forming healthy followership that crosses racial and cultural differences. As college president, it was often the case that the students who came from homogenous white high schools had a more difficult time when their student body president was black, their team captain was Hispanic, or their resident assistant was from a different country. Of course, some learned quickly that such differences shouldn't be an obstacle but a learning experience; others retreated as they weren't able to get out of their comfort zones.

One of the most positive trends (with some detractors, unfortunately) has been workplace training in areas of diversity and anti-racism. While the various approaches may differ, they all help attendees understand themselves—culture, history, attitudes—and others of differing cultures and races. Understanding others is the first step in following well.

While I've participated in such trainings, the best lessons in my lifetime were taught directly to me by African-Americans. Long ago, I had an African-American colleague who one time, in a moment of frustration with me, said "you just don't get it!" That was a breakthrough moment, because it was a direct, unavoidable assessment someone made of me. Fortunately, between my wanting to learn and my colleague's drive, I went on to learn much from her, and our work together flourished. At another point in my cross-cultural development, I was an elder in our urban church, and I was paired with an African-American woman deacon. It was our church's practice for these pairs to visit families in the church, listening to their hopes and concerns and spurring them on in their faith journeys. Loutisha was about twenty years older than me and truly a saint. I learned to follow her lead in these visits, given her spiritual wisdom as expressed through her African-American culture and related approach to faith. I and the families we visited learned much about reliance on God through thick and thin.

In a similar way, national events—as sad and discouraging as they can be—can wake up some to the challenges they need to overcome. The tragic deaths of Trayvon Martin, George Floyd, Ahmaud Arbery, or any other young black males or females can help one grow, understanding more thoroughly racial injustice and the important meaning of Black Lives Matter.

Unfortunately, often the opposite reaction occurs: where prejudice is unchanged, and all kinds of cognitive gymnastics occur so to rationalize the death or racist situation. I recall a conversation with a co-worker who, when learning that the Michigan State Police were found to disproportionally stop African Americans than others, simply concluded that black males speed more than others.[3] I shared with him some stories of our black sons' encounters with traffic stops due to profiling, but his racist perspective seemingly did not change. In many cases, the challenge is simply moved to a different agenda. Critical race theory has become the archenemy of some, and most frustrating is when those seeking to ban it don't even understand it.[4]

More than frustrating is when Christians are behind these efforts, assuming that sin is only an individual phenomenon without opening their minds (or their Bibles) to understand that God sent his son to save the world—including the renewal of social structures and systems. For example, evangelical leader Josh McDowell spoke at a conference of Christian counselors, rejecting

3. Eggert, "Michigan State Police Disproportionately Stop Black Drivers."
4. Ray and Gibbons, "Why Are States Banning Critical Race Theory?"

critical race theory saying that CRT "negates all the biblical teaching about racism—because it focuses on systems rather than the sins of the human heart."[5] Followers of Christian leaders such as McDowell are not only being short-changed on understanding the gospel call, they are being maladaptively trained to follow poorly in society as well.

False dichotomies such as the one voiced by McDowell are unfortunately alive and well in the church. As a denominational leader, most often members within the denomination would call or e-mail me about something a church leader had posted or a declaration I had signed that sought to expose the sin of racism at a societal level. The classic criticism was a more shielded analysis than that which McDowell offered. These critics would say the church is prohibited from stepping into the public square in such a way. While these critics seemingly could recognize both individual sin and systemic/institutional sin, they were interpreting incorrectly a prohibition, one that requires nonprofit organizations in the US from supporting political candidates. Others would use phrases borrowed from the confederacy or any other era where slavery or racism was tolerated by the church: "It's just too divisive of an issue." "If it's preached from the pulpit we'll be sliding into liberal social gospel approaches." Or, "The church's primary role is to focus on individuals, not institutions or society." Of course, when I would suggest that the church should then not speak in the public square about abortion, my comment would be met with silence or a quick end to the conversation.

In sum, one of the key reasons that following well fails to occur cross-culturally or across racial divides in U.S. society is that key social institutions such as schools and churches fail to address the problems. Further, opponents of Critical Race Theory are making it difficult to teach about systemic and institutional racism in schools and many white evangelical churches have developed cases of selective mutism with most social ills other than abortion. Where does that leave leaders who must lead with followers of a variety of cultural and racial backgrounds?

5. Smietana, "Josh McDowell Steps Back," para. 4.

Following the Leader—The Role of Culture and Race

Many of those leaders are white, and many, like myself, are white males. As such, we know some of our followers are racially and culturally different from us. This knowledge and our responses can range from patronizing comments to intentional inclusion. Be careful when you hear pronouns such as "they," for often that is a clue to the white leader's insensitive presumption that he knows what "they" are like, what "they" need, and how "they" should find him as their caring and understanding leader. In both of my positions of leadership—college and denomination—I insisted on the leadership team being multicultural. For if a leader's leadership colleagues reflect a different race or culture than the leader, missteps and maladjusted attitudes get caught earlier while true appreciations for cultural differences will develop among the team and throughout those who follow, regardless of cultural or racial background.

A very fine colleague of mine—and the one who took my place as our denomination's chief executive officer when I left—brought incredible gifts to leadership with previous wide-ranging experiences in corporate America. Furthermore, in addition to his journey of leadership as an African-American male, he also knew the immigrant experience, having come to the US from what was then British Guyana as a late teen. While commanding the respect and admiration of followers particularly from underrepresented communities in the church, he was not at all naïve about the challenge of leading the largely white membership of the denomination. While his stories are his to tell, he was always intentional in dress (a jacket and tie), deliberate in treating all with fairness and respect, and purposeful in listening well. He served the entire denomination so very well.

As I watch others from various cultural and racial backgrounds lead among followers who are mainly white, I have seen, too, a commanding sense of graciousness and even-temperament despite the subtle and sometimes not so-subtle racial attitudes and microaggressions they face. Michelle Obama put it well, providing the commencement address at Tuskegee University's graduation undoubtedly shaped by her own experiences:

Followership

The world won't always see you in those caps and gowns. They won't know how hard you worked and how much you sacrificed to make it to this day—the countless hours you spent studying to get this diploma, the multiple jobs you worked to pay for school, the times you had to drive home and take care of your grandma, the evenings you gave up to volunteer at a food bank or organize a campus fundraiser. They don't know that part of you. Instead, they will make assumptions about who they think you are based on their limited notion of the world. And my husband and I know how frustrating that experience can be. We've both felt the sting of those daily slights throughout our entire lives—the folks who crossed the street in fear of their safety; the clerks who kept a close eye on us in all those department stores; the people at formal events who assumed we were the "help"—and those who have questioned our intelligence, our honesty, even our love of this country. And I know that these little indignities are obviously nothing compared to what folks across the country are dealing with every single day—those nagging worries that you're going to get stopped or pulled over for absolutely no reason; the fear that your job application will be overlooked because of the way your name sounds; the agony of sending your kids to schools that may no longer be separate, but are far from equal; the realization that no matter how far you rise in life, how hard you work to be a good person, a good parent, a good citizen—for some folks, it will never be enough.[6]

While her ending comment provides a degree of fatalism, the seeming reality is that some will always be mired in their own racism. As for herself and her husband, the approach they took is so nicely summed up in the phrase we heard her say often, beginning first at the Democratic Convention when her husband was selected as the party's candidate for president: "When they go low, we go high."[7]

---

6. Badger, "Michelle Obama on Being Black," paras. 4–6.
7. Abcarian, "When They Go Low," para. 8.

Concluding Reflections

Cross-cultural and trans-racial living is filled with challenges. And such has been our life, with one biracial, one white and five black grandchildren, and six black and six white adult sons and daughters and their spouses (I honestly had to look at the family Christmas picture to be sure of this count!).

Sometimes these challenges have come from outside of our family such as when our sons have had to sit through the indignity of police racial profiling stops or having an athletic director fail to understand why they were not willing to shake hands with opponents who called them the n-word during a soccer match. While these occasions can be disheartening for us, the white parents, how deeply the wounds go for our sons is hard to measure.

Even more challenging are when issues arise from within our family. As mentioned previously, issues of time can derail family gatherings. Moreover, consciously or unconsciously, comments made about the differences in racial group membership within the family can quickly spring out of seemingly nowhere. When someone says "my white mama," it's often in fun, but it can make any or all of us stop in our tracks and seek to understand whether there's a deeper meaning at that given moment. Other times, the racial difference leads to a strategic request. When one of my Ethiopian sons asks me to join him for some formal meeting, the reason can be the need to be taken more seriously when there's a white parent in tow.

Indeed, there are times when I just don't get it. But I'm always open to learning. A risk of course is that in a trans-racial family such as ours, I have more agency as an adult to take a step back "to learn." Especially earlier in life, our black kids in particular probably had no such opportunity. While we have tried to ensure that schooling and church life have included diversity, the settings have always been predominantly white. One incident, in particular, demonstrated the importance of diversity as we approached moving from Chicago to Grand Rapids. Our youngest (Ethiopian) son would need to transfer to a new school to begin tenth grade. The first school we visited seemed okay, but there was no significant

Followership

reaction from Fekadu. At the second school we visited, the Dean of Students—an African-American male—greeted us at the door. That automatically sealed the school choice decision for Fekadu—whose decision it needed to be.

I wonder sometimes if our kids—both white and black—have been better prepared to be followers in their still unfolding adult lives. I suspect our white kids have had greater and more intimate exposure to diversity of culture and race than most, leaving them with the potential to follow well whatever leader they may encounter. I would hope, too, that our black kids, by virtue of the whiteness of their adoptive family, would be prepared to follow whatever leader they encounter. Yet, the burden is and will be for our black kids and grandchildren, as expressed so realistically in Michelle Obama's address at the Tuskegee commencement ceremony.

An advantage of adopting older children, particularly in our case, relates to culture. Of the three, the two oldest were culturally Ethiopian through and through. Even the youngest's fluency in his native Amharic language never lessened. Moreover, during the first six or seven years, we made sure they made it back to Ethiopia at least every other year if not more frequently. In addition, while phone cards allowed them to keep in touch with friends and family when they were first adopted, the internet now allows daily contact or more!

The historic model for immigration was assimilation. We've been able to witness in our three adopted kids something different, something I'll call additive: learning American culture while keeping their Ethiopian culture. While at times they might feel, as many third culture kids do, uncertain as to their "real" culture, they are so richly blessed to be fully bilingual with competencies in two cultures.

Would Barb and I do it all over again? For certain! Our unusual and sometimes challenging family is such a blessing. In my work both in the college setting and the denominational setting, my ability to work and connect internationally was incredibly enhanced. Our friendships with so many others have deepened—both with similar "internationalized" American families and with those from around the globe. And finally, we have developed a foretaste of the kingdom yet coming with those from every nation, tribe, and tongue as described in Rev 7:9.

4

Following the Leader

Into Adulthood

EVERY STAGE OF LIFE involves following well. Think of the two-year old who needs to follow the parent's lead when the word "no" is used. Or when that child enters preschool or kindergarten and it is necessary to follow the teacher's lead. Then, too, when that child begins playing a musical instrument in the band or becomes a member on a school athletic team—following the director or coach is essential. High school brings more choice in following, as some seek leadership in positions in student government while others are content with following the crowd.

But one of the most crucial stages where followership is required occurs when moving into adulthood. Buckets full of choices about who and what late teens and young adults will follow present themselves. I've noticed with my own children, as they move through this stage, that the choices they encountered required, at times, abrupt changes. Certainly, leaving high school involves choices: university study or the world of work. However, most teens simply follow a trajectory they've been on—a trajectory shaped by parents, classmates, and other significant adults.

When the choice is university study, it functions as a continuation of followership learned in high school: class schedules

Following the Leader—Into Adulthood

to follow, teachers to follow, peers to follow, instructions to follow, a calendar of school and vacation to follow, and the like. While it is true the university years are less prescribed than high school, unmitigated followership continues until the last year or two. As internships are needed, decisions about further study are considered, and job hunting begins, finally a young adult begins to take an active role in followership by making decisions about what pathway to follow.

I think of two of our daughters who nearly went directly into graduate school. After they obtained their master's degrees, it seemed they were fairly certain about the kind of job they wanted—following their goals, instead of following someone else. When I think of four other of my children, they "launched" after their bachelor's degrees, and for each there seemed to be initial times of greater wondering and wandering.

Notice what goes on here regardless of the launch time. A level of experience and maturity is needed to not only follow one's goals, but also to define them. What are the common missteps? There are a number of things I'd like to address for this age group.

First, it is an error to assume someone else will provide you your goals—even though it's the case there usually will be someone in your life who would readily oblige. At first blush, it makes sense to receive your goals from someone else, because during the previous dozen plus years, someone else usually provided you goals to some degree. It can take some time to now realize whose responsibility it is and then to develop them.

If your preparatory steps (high school, college, or graduate school) provided a specific career goal (electrician, nurse, or counselor, for example), the goals have in effect been given to you. The only decisions are about where to live, what subspeciality you desire, or in what context you wish to work. For example, one of daughters graduated with a master's of social work degree. Her decision was to follow her goals to work in an area of macro-social work practice. The job market defined the rest. In contrast, another example is one of our sons who graduated with a math degree and a physics minor. It took him longer to identify his goals and even

Followership

though he has found his niche in the world of work, he still returns to his goals from time to time, deciding whether to change them.

A second misstep after university study is to go on following the crowd as you did during your university years—even though the crowd you've followed has dissipated. I see this in those who can't give up the video-game habits developed in their dorm rooms—presumably a social activity at the time. Or those for whom every weekend night means time at the bars and night clubs, even though most of their college crowd has discontinued such behavior as they have moved into the world of work and responsibilities. A subset of this misstep is to continue to ignore church, as is common during college. While there is no specific intention to ignore church, the habit of sleeping in on Sundays takes hold. While discontinuing church affiliation and attendance doesn't mean a loss of faith, it may result in failing to deepen and grow in faith; in addition, it may cause you to lose a significant peer group that would reinforce values you hold.

Another area where followership can go awry as formal education concludes is seen when following narrows to just one or two things—again without intention. For example, I've seen former students move out of college and very soon be following the American Dream in a variety of forms—where to live, what kind of job/salary is chosen, what kind of vehicle is purchased, and the like. A variation of this nearly single-minded followership is making your job central—leaving little time for other relationships or activities, and turning down other pathways of followership because they would interfere with the all-important job.

Of course, the opposite can also happen, as the student lives in a state of denial, avoiding that he or she must make choices/develop goals to follow; instead, the habits continue: sleeping on your friend's couch, accepting a low paying job because the work requirements aren't taxing, going to mom and dad over and over for money in emergencies (which crops up often in this kind of lifestyle).

A similar misstep that can happen during these years is to become addicted to freedom. I see this in young adults who can't stop traveling the world, even if it's for doing good. Stopping world

Following the Leader—Into Adulthood

travel to get serious with a potential partner, to become focused on vocation, or to put down roots in groups and community requires intentionality—following something different from following the desire of being "free to be me."

A final potential misstep at this phase of life is making significant unfortunate choices in followership. I've spoken with parents who are agonizing over their son or daughter's unfortunate decision about following. Consider the charismatic leader (religious or non-religious) with warning signs so clearly evident to all but the young person. Think about the person who finds pot-smoking or drinking to be the lifestyle to follow. You can think of specific examples, but core to all is the willingness to wholeheartedly follow someone or something that ends up shaping and providing you *all* of your (unsatisfying or minimalistic) goals, *all* of your (void of creativity and exploration) daily patterns, and *all* of your (delusional or avoidance of) beliefs.

What's the answer to making these years a good transition? Steven Garber understands these challenges and provides helpful insight as the subtitle of his book suggests: "Weaving together belief and behavior during the university years."[1] Focusing on moral development, he suggests that during these years when moral meaning is formed young adults need to make choices in three areas:

1. Develop a worldview that can make sense of life, facing the challenge of truth and coherence in an increasingly pluralistic world;
2. Pursue a relationship with a teacher whose life incarnates the worldview the student is learning to embrace;
3. Commit themselves to others who have chosen to live their lives embedded in that same worldview, journeying together in truth after the vision of a coherent and meaningful life.[2]

Notice that Garber focuses on *worldview, relationship,* and *commitment,* and while he doesn't use the language of followership,

---

1. Garber, *Fabric of Faithfulness*.
2. Garber, *Fabric of Faithfulness*, 171.

Followership

we can understand these three dimensions as conscious choices to follow in worldview, relationship, and commitment.

Before proceeding further, we need to understand *worldview*. While it can be defined a number of ways, I appreciate the definition of worldview by Brian Walsh and J. Richard Middleton: "They [worldviews] are not systems of thought, like theologies or philosophies. Rather, world views are perceptual frameworks. They are ways of seeing."[3] And then later: "Our world view determines our values. It helps us interpret the world around us. It sorts out what is important from what is not, what is of highest value from what is the least. A world view, then, provides a model *of the world* which guides its adherents *in the world*."[4]

Walsh and Middleton speak of worldview as providing a guiding function. I maintain that a worldview will bring about a drive toward relationships and commitments. The highest level of relationships—such as a teacher that helps shape you and your future or commitments that help you live-out your values—comes from a worldview that is other-centered, using a secular humanist concept. Far better is to rely on a biblical value of loving God, then neighbor, and finally self (see Mark 12; also book one of Augustine's *On Christian Doctrine*).

But even more than that, if God is at the center (and then neighbor and finally self), you begin to understand how the world works and your place in it. Consider the two parts of this understanding.

First, explaining how the world works doesn't mean we're answering how the world goes round, giving an economic or ecological lecture or discussing global cultures and histories. Rather, I advocate using the biblical framework that God created the world (*creation*); through our first parents sin entered, making our world so fallen (*the fall*) that God sent his son Jesus to redeem the world (*redemption*) and finally, that ultimately the entire cosmos will be restored to God's original intent (*restoration*). (For more on this theme, see books like Cornelius Plantinga's 2002 work, *Engaging God's World*.)

---

3. Walsh and Middleton, *Transforming Vision*, 17.
4. Walsh and Middleton, *Transforming Vision*, 32.

Then, using this biblical framework, we begin to better understand that which we see or perceive. The Holocaust? Fallenness to a horrible degree. A beautiful flower? God's wonderful creation. Committing one's life to Christ? Redemption. Fighting climate change? On the road to restoration.

Once you begin using your worldview to understand or perceive the world (hopefully based on a biblical foundation), then you can work toward finding your place in it. Maybe you'll look for a career in corrections, understanding the need for individuals to move from fallenness to redemption. Perhaps you'll work on coral reefs, seeking to restore the oceans to what God intended in his creation.

More than vocation, your worldview also provides values—values about what is priceless and what is worthy. Is chasing after the American Dream really worthy? Is the end result priceless?

And finally, Walsh and Middleton note, "World views are always shared; they are communal."[5] Living and seeing with a worldview is not a solo act. It involves others—those with similar worldviews where together relationships are formed and deepened while commitments are formed, challenged, and refined.

So, again, how do we avoid the missteps moving into adulthood and knowing what and who to follow:

1. Identify your worldview and explore its (hopefully biblical) foundation; then understand better what you see and your place in the world. Thus, you'll develop goals, knowing better what and who to follow.

2. Develop deep relationships with those who have similar worldviews (this doesn't mean excising those with differing worldviews out of your life), and journey together through worship and church affiliation, by means of critical and challenging conversations and via explicitly and purposefully identifying personal and group goals.

3. Form commitments springing out of your worldview and with the help of others in these important relationships.

5. Walsh and Middleton, *Transforming Vision*, 32.

Followership

Maybe some in your group are committed to orphans; assist them in their commitment by helping them as they pursue adoption. Perhaps you've seized on a personal commitment to eating healthy and exercising; your group should encourage and even join you in this commitment.

Notice what is beginning to happen. There's little room for avoidance, and there will be those who help you steer clear of following unhealthy habits, movements or leaders. Your values come clearly into sight, and they begin to shape who and what you follow, be it concern for neighbors nearby and far away, identifying your privilege and moving towards racial reconciliation, or using your financial resources not only to sustain your life, but also the lives of those in need.

My wife and I can look back with delight as we notice what former students are up to—not following the crowd, but shaping their lives in ways that reflect their worldviews, that are rich in relationships, and reflect extraordinary commitments.

We think of the student who married cross-culturally and together she and her husband are pursuing community development in Guatemala. A shared worldview, a deep marriage relationship that invites others to become engaged with them in ministry, and an enduring commitment to each other, to fellow church members, and to their community.

Another pair of students babysat for us during their college years. Today, they both serve at their inner-city church, developing relationships among the lost, the least, and the last. Moreover, every year, they spend a month exercising their gifts of medicine in Rwanda.

I think of students who were part of a travel group I led to South Africa and Malawi. There were so many eye-opening aspects to the experience. Staying in an AIDS hospice each evening for lodging. Seeing parts of Johannesburg abandoned due to white flight with African immigrants settling in the empty buildings. Going on to Malawi where local entrepreneurs were guided by our students in business principles. Today one of these former students is a representative in his state's legislature.

One of my favorite students is Emmanuel. His parents had fled their native Rwanda due to the 1994 genocide, and he was born in Tanzania. He, his siblings, and his parents waited there in a refugee camp for years. They were like millions of other refugees in our world today, waiting and depending upon decision makers far away to determine their future. In Emmanuel's case, after many years of waiting, the family was given permission to come to the U.S., ending up in Boise, Idaho. From there, Emmanuel found Trinity Christian College where he chose to be a psychology major with a goal to counsel prison inmates. What's the connection? Emmanuel knows something about waiting—as do prison inmates—and he has already demonstrated excellence in building relationships and distinction in the commitments he forms on campus and beyond. The bonus? This young man is a beautiful reminder of God's abiding relationship with those created in his image—something undoubtedly shaped by his parents' worldview while waiting in a refugee camp. They named their son Emmanuel—God with us!

Concluding Reflections

While I've addressed missteps in this chapter as well as reflected upon those I've known in a variety of contexts, I have to confess that some stories, too personal to share, tug at my heart strings. Especially for parents, a son or daughter who makes dead-end choices while seeking to launch can leave parents carrying a heavy burden and fully exasperated. This description by Ferris Jabr captures it well:

> In the opening scene of Lena Dunham's HBO series *Girls*, the Horvaths tell their 24-year-old daughter Hannah that they will no longer support her—or, as her mother puts it: "No. More. *Money*." A recent college graduate, Hannah has been living in Brooklyn, completing an unpaid internship and working on a series of personal essays. The Horvaths intend to give Hannah "one final push" toward, presumably, a lifestyle that more closely resembles

adulthood. Hannah protests. Her voice quavers. She tells her parents that she does not want to see them the following day, even though they are leaving town soon: "I have work and then I have a dinner thing and then I am busy—trying to become who I am."[6]

The author goes on, reviewing research that indicates a very important time for the development of brain structure and function is from twelve to twenty-five with continued but less significant development throughout the twenties. My point is simple. Those of us are who are parents often feel like the Horvaths, but we need to be more patient during this time period for our sons and daughters.

The issue isn't only brain development. Sociologists point to how adolescence is extending. Bret Stetka explores this phenomenon, suggesting that twenty-five may be the new eighteen.[7] His review reveals that while children from large families or lower affluence launch into adulthood at the approximate stage of earlier generations, those from affluence are often more delayed. Affluence allows youth to delay their launch, assuming there's plenty of time to do so.

Whether reading this section as a parent or a twenty-something, the missteps reviewed in this chapter remain significant. A too-simplistic yet often helpful phrase is that past behavior predicts future behavior. Avoiding employment, relationships, or commitments becomes a habit that's hard to shake; following the wrong crowd or impulses is a pattern that too quickly becomes enduring. So the role of bystanders is to provide suggestions—one at a time.

In our own family, this challenge has presented itself and confirms what Stetka reports. As mentioned before, our adoption of three siblings occurred when they were older. Orphan life had been difficult and the launch of the older two fits the pattern of where their growing up was in the context of less affluence—for that was the majority of their lives. Their launch, as a result, demonstrated goal-directed behavior, hard work, and striving for

6. Jabr, "Neuroscience of 20-Somethings," para. 1
7. Steka, "Extended Adolescence," para. 8.

independence. The youngest, however, having spent more time in our family than as an orphan as did his older siblings, has experienced affluence the majority of his life. And so, his launch has been more delayed. While I may feel like Mr. Horvath, I need to recognize the importance of brain development in the twenties and the sociological context unique to him. My approach has been to tackle one goal at a time. Maybe it's just encouraging a daily trip to the gym—and patiently waiting for that behavior to become habit. Maybe it's filling a gas tank with no request for reimbursement when that tank will enable meeting another goal. The bottom line is this: don't push but together identify goals and address them one at a time.

5

Following the Leader

In the Workplace

THE WORKPLACE, WITH ALL its organizational charts, job descriptions, and supervisory roles, ought to be the place where followership and leadership runs smoothly and without confusion. However, the workplace is not exempt from troubles and, in fact, it's often the proving grounds for the rest of life.

In the previous chapters, numerous references to the workplace and followership have already been made, perhaps due to its centrality to all of our lives and the place where working out followership and leadership is required. We've looked at narcissism, the pathway to leadership, and gender differences. In addition, we've addressed culture, mentioning parts it plays in the workplace. And, as mentioned previously, the field of organizational studies has focused on courageous followership and provided three models of courageous followership.

First is Robert Kelly's Followership Model in which he suggests there are two aspects of followership — thinking for oneself and one's attitude.[1] While the categories are self-evident by their titles, the last—the *Star Follower*—this person, after thinking

---

1. Kelly, *Power of Followership*.

critically, "has earned the right to be heard because he or she always give their best effort with positive can-do attitude."

Second is Ira Chaleff's Courageous Followership Model found in his book, *The Courageous Follower: Standing Up to and for Our Leaders*.[2] His four quadrants of followership focus on concepts of supportiveness and challenge as shown here:

High Support

	Quadrant II	Quadrant I	
Low	IMPLEMENTER	PARTNER	High
Challenge	Quadrant IV	Quadrant III	Challenge
	RESOURCE	INDIVIDUALIST	

Low Support

The best quadrant is the first, *Partner*. "These types of followers take full responsibility for their own as well as the leader's behaviors and act accordingly. They give their whole heart to the corporate vision and the initiatives of the leader, but are open and honest enough to speak up when something doesn't mesh with the best interests of the organization."

The final model also has four quadrants and is offered by Rodger Adair in his 4-D Followership Model.[3] He focuses on three variables: job satisfaction, likelihood to stay, and productivity. The resultant four types of followers relate to these three variables. *Doers* are high in productivity but low in the other two variables. The *Disengaged* are unlikely to depart (because they don't like change nor do they desire improvement) but are low in the other two variables. The *Disgruntled* are low in all three areas. Finally, the *Disciple* is someone who is high in all three areas which includes being team-focused and being willing to give up individual opportunities to help others.

2. Chaleff, *Courageous Follower*, 67–87.
3. Riggio et al., *Art of Followership*, 137–54.

Followership

Let's look at the best follower as explained from these three theorists: the *Star Follower* who has a can-do attitude and whose voice commands respect, the *Partner* who is all-in but does not lose his or her critical perspective because of commitment to the organization, and the *Disciple* who is team-focused to the point of putting others before self. Much of this fits with what we already covered: committing to the organization enough to speak up (a rough parallel to commitment to God) and concern for teammates (parallel to loving your neighbor).

With these theoretical perspectives, we can look at shortcomings and correctives for those who follow in the workplace. And then we will look at the need for followership among leaders, hoping that you will benefit, whatever role you fill.

Shifting focus, I've already mentioned the passive-aggressive tendencies for some followers to use in the workplace. While my example focused on culture and gender, the following shortcomings may or may not cross genders or cultures.

In my experience, one of the deadliest unhealthy behaviors of followers in the workplace is that of complaining. Whether the complaints focus on the boss ("he doesn't know anything"), the task ("it's impossible to do what we've been asked to do"), or the context ("it's too hot in here"), complaining might seem to get things off someone's chest, so to speak, but my experience is that complainers continue to complain. The effect is demoralizing for those who listen—either because they pick up the refrain or because they feel trapped working with a complainer. This fits with Adair's *Disgruntled* category who is low in job satisfaction, likelihood to stay, and productivity.

A close relative to complaining is to hang so tightly to one's job description that often a refrain is heard: "That's not my job." Notice how the word "my" immediately can reflect egocentrism and counters any sense of teamwork. When I spent a short time driving for a rental car company, I encountered this over and over, becoming demoralized and trapped. After driving a car to the airport, ready for rental, some problem was found: missed dirt, bugs on the windshield, or the like. Most frequently I heard "not in my job description." Again, I turn to Adair whose category *disengaged* fits: likely to stay but low in productivity and job satisfaction.

Complaining and staking out what lies outside one's role can easily lead to passive-aggressive behaviors or worse. Between my junior and senior year of college, I worked on an assembly line in a factory making seats for automobiles. Once a line shut down, it was interesting to watch how slowly the factory workers addressed the problem and restored production. Worse than passive-aggressive, workers were also known to purposively sabotage a line to shut it down.

Somewhere between complaint and passive-aggressive acts falls death by a thousand cuts. Utilizing all kinds of words and actions, some workers follow the leader in such a critical and negative way that it extinguishes joy, respect, and motivation. It can even lead a leader to leave.

The results contribute to a toxic workplace. Liz Ryan provides eleven indicators of such a workplace:

- The first sign of a toxic culture is a feeling you will pick up when you spend time in a workplace where people don't communicate, don't smile, don't joke and don't reinforce one another. You will notice that interactions are more formal than friendly and that no one seems happy to be working there. A visitor or newcomer will feel the dark energy while the employees seem oblivious to it. That makes sense—the fish can't see how murky the water in their fishbowl has become!

- The second sign of a toxic workplace is that people are very concerned about titles, job descriptions and levels in the hierarchy. When you meet someone new in the organization, they'll be quick to tell you their title and status. Power (the conferred kind associated with a job title or connections to high-level leaders) is more important to the people working in the toxic environment than the mission they're supposedly pursuing.

- The third sign of a toxic culture is that rules and policies are very important. It's more important than the good judgment of your teammates, their combined

Followership

decades of experience or the rich context of the situation you're dealing with. Everybody is afraid of getting in trouble for breaking the rules, and so they keep their heads low and try not to step out of line.

- The fourth sign of a toxic workplace is that managers and employees make up two completely separate groups that seldom interact. When they do interact, it's a one-way communication in which the manager tells the underling what to do. There's no other give-and-take conversation or collaboration between management and everybody else.

- The fifth sign of a toxic culture is that while it's well known that employees are unhappy, nobody talks about it openly. HR people may be off-site or just not involved, or they may be frustratingly chirpy and ineffectual as they pretend along with everybody else not to notice the dark and rotten culture. In any case, they are not a resource for employees.

- The sixth sign of a toxic culture is that there is much talk about infractions and demerits but little to no recognition of extraordinary effort or triumphs.

- The seventh sign of a toxic workplace is that people do not speak up even when they are presented with impossible goals, ridiculous plans or patently stupid ideas they are expected to implement. They say nothing, but later they complain to their friends about the stupid ideas and foolish goals.

- The eighth sign of a toxic culture is that the informal grapevine is many times more effective as a communications network than any type of official company communication.

- The ninth sign of a toxic culture is that employees have little to no latitude in performing their jobs. Every procedure is spelled out for them. If they are rewarded at all, they are rewarded for hitting their goals and following the rules, but never for having breakout ideas or pushing for much-needed changes—activities that could get them fired.

Following the Leader—In the Workplace

- The 10th sign of a toxic culture is that fear is palpable in the environment. Doors slam and whispered conversations take place in stairwells. Everybody is concerned with his or her own spot on the company's constantly-shifting, internal stock index. They ask one another "Does the big boss like me? What did he say about me?" and fret and worry about who's up and who's down.
- The final sign of a toxic workplace is that there is no community. The few people who laugh and joke with one another get suspicious sideways looks from people who are too afraid to let their hair down.[4]

Yikes. The list of characteristics of a toxic workplace seems overwhelming. But like with most things, change begins with a single step. Followers who complain, cite the limits of their job descriptions, or resort to passive aggressiveness have a responsibility to change their behavior, no matter who is their leader and how toxic is the workplace. Followers of Jesus on the road of sanctification have the power, found in the gifts of the Spirit, to change even if their leader and context do not.

Almost more importantly, what does one do if he or she is in a toxic workplace but doesn't contribute to its toxicity? Maybe one person demonstrating joy, teamwork, and going above and beyond will influence not only other workers, but also the leaders. But even if such influence doesn't occur, the individual is responsible for his or her own behavior before the Lord. Remember the words oft-times attributed to St. Francis of Assisi: "Preach the gospel at all times, and if necessary, use words." In other words, model what you believe, and I'd suggest in the workplace, keep words to a minimum in challenging situations.

Part of modeling means staying away from the gripe sessions or not voicing the "it's not in my job description," but, instead, concentrating on how you are part of the team—Adair's Disciple. Sometimes it may feel like covering for the weakest link. Instead of thinking "if I cover for him/her, that's unjust—he/she needs to do better," focus on you. Whether that weak-link person is having a

---

4. Ryan, "Ten Unmistakable Signs of a Toxic Culture."

Followership

bad day or is simply negative and purposeful in his/her poor performance, you are the one that needs to shine, loving a neighbor/teammate who really prefers to be unlovable.

More broadly, avoid taking part in the toxicity in any form. It can be tough and may require looking neither to one side or the other, but glue your eyes straight ahead, doing your job the best you can. I believe you will soon find those who are encouraged by your work as well as those who resent your work. Your job in following is not to win popularity prizes, but maybe you'll find a handful of positive coworkers who, together, will shift the tide.

Remember, too, that followers follow a leader. Even if your leader is part of the toxicity or has a handful of annoying characteristics, your goal isn't to change your leader. Rather, your goal should be to communicate with your leader. The best communication doesn't come after a problem or in response to challenges. Rather, your communicating with your leader comes best when there's neither a heightened sense of anxiety nor a crisis in the background. Instead, communicate with honesty and respect, as would a *Partner* (Chaleff) or a *Star Follower* (Kelly). Don't dump, but focus on one or two things. You don't know the multitude of variables confronting your leader. Be filled with grace.

In addition, if there are a few others as mentioned above, communicate together—but rehearse first! While I'm not necessarily advocating union organizing, I am suggesting that a multitude of voices communicating in unison can be very helpful.

While in the final analysis the leaders have the authority to change things, each of us has the responsibility to work for change, avoiding the traps of wallowing in toxicity in any form and, instead, communicating and collaborating, when possible, with grace and truth.

Before we leave the topic of shortcomings, we should focus on leaders. I suspect anybody who has been in the workplace could write this section! Nevertheless, consider these facets which you may have encountered:

First, in the earlier chapter on the role of gender, the movement of narcissists to CEO happens, and as mentioned before, the impact can be the creation of an individualistic culture in the organization, the reduction of collaborating and integrity among the workforce, and making rash and risky decisions that ultimately harm the company.

Second, an unscientifically derived form of narcissism is the person who likes the title, loves getting quoted, and succeeds at public events—but really doesn't have interest in the day-to-day responsibilities of leadership. Like me, you have probably experienced this kind of leader. I call this type of personality the *prince* or *princess*. This leader doesn't deserve to be king or queen but they are ascending only due to the fluke of ancestry or some other factor. While it was always easy for me to be gracious toward the fellow leader who was a bit behind (due to being overworked!), it was far more difficult to show grace to another prince who preferred to woo his royal subjects in the hope of becoming king rather than ensuring his work was completed.

Third, we may have experienced the leader who holds his or her position as a result of the Peter Principle: that people are promoted to their level of incompetence. I find this happens often to the good person who has stayed in the organization. Thus, when promoted to leader, his or her experiences haven't had opportunities to broaden by working in other places or situations. While it is true that a program of continuing education may improve this leader, the often or occasional slipup is wearisome for those that follow.

Fourth is the leader who lacks having all the tools in the toolkit. I find this kind of leader often in the world of work that's so dependent upon technology. I recall in one setting that after a higher education leader departed, the staff found that his computer had never been hooked up to a printer. While he had adapted, it was clear that he was technologically challenged. I recall another leader in higher education who was so very gifted in her work, but was fearful of continuing education or other means that would bring her to the cutting edge of her field. While both of these examples—and there could be more—demonstrate different ways leaders can have a missing component in their tool box, I find that whatever the missing component is, the attitude is often similar:

Followership

It worked for me in the past, so it will work for me in the future. In other words, this person believes new skills and approaches aren't needed; unfortunately for such leaders, the world keeps changing.

Finally, there are leaders who knows the roles and responsibilities of their workers, but instead of allowing them to fulfill their responsibilities (sometime even making modification they have discovered), the leader micromanages. This can take many forms: stepping into a worker's assignment and taking over, checking up over and over on someone's work, reminding them again and again what they already know, instructing a worker on details that may reflect the leader's preference but have no bearing on the results, and the list goes on.

In some of my performance evaluations as a college president I was identified as a micromanager. I can still get defensive about this assessment (as might come through in the following paragraph), for I thought my direct, hands-on involvement in many areas was warranted in at least two ways. First, the college I served had a small endowment and little room for financial error. So, I was hands-on in finances. Even when we built a building, I would visit two furniture manufacturers about 100 miles away to find bargains, coupling the trips with other purposes. Yes, I could have sent someone else, but finding bargains seemed less important to many in the face of their day-to-day workloads. Second, I tended to step into day-to-day operations and throw new ideas in the mix. Working with faculty and staff members with significant longevity meant they hadn't experienced other campuses and ways of strategizing. So, while it may have seemed intrusive for me to suggest we start offering summer classes, it turned out to be a significant help to students and to the bottom line. Similarly, when I suggested partnering with a nonprofit urban educational assistance group in the city, it took new behaviors and methods for staff and faculty to make this work. Again, it was an overall positive for students and the bottom line.

One last topic needs to be addressed: followership in leadership. We need to be reminded that the leader, as mentioned in chapter one, is never without some higher group or board to

Following the Leader—In the Workplace

whom he or she answers. Thus, leaders must always be attentive to following well, and the following list is intended to help leaders achieve that goal.

First, leaders need to be evaluated if they are to follow the direction set by the board and the goals of the organization's strategic plan. As a leader, the college I worked for used a 360° evaluation process—modifying it as necessary—to best understand my strengths and weaknesses. That meant that a wide range of individuals contributed to my evaluation, some working closely with me and others without such day-to-day familiarity. In addition, I was always asked for my own self-evaluation.

This approach connects nicely to the Johari window, a device developed in 1955 by Joseph Luft and Harry Ingham (Johari is a title derived from combine parts of their first names). It's a window into the self with four panes. The first pane includes both what I see about myself and what others see of me. The second is what others see about me but I can't see myself. In the third pane, I see the part of me that others can't see. The fourth pane is the hidden self not seen by myself or by others.

A 360° evaluation provides the leader with the second pane—what others see about me but I can't see myself—my blind spot. It is the place to begin the corrective journey, either by forming goals individually or with others contributing, and then reflecting on progress at least quarterly.

Earlier I mentioned the lack of a key tool or tools in the leader's bag of tools. Whether this lack is identified via the 360° process or other means, it is incumbent upon the leader to address his or her deficiencies. I recall a new president boot camp I attended, with sessions offered by various college presidents. I attended this a year after I began, believing that if I took it the summer before beginning (as most attendees did), I wouldn't know what I didn't know. My hunch proved correct, and I found it to be an incredibly important experience, particularly in areas where my toolset was incomplete—federal and state law relative to private higher education, finances and debt ratios, and many other smaller items. As testimony to the importance of this learning experience for me, in my eleventh year of being a college president, I was still consulting with the person who had led the learning sequence relative to finances and debt ratios

Second, it is important that a leader takes advantage of continuing education opportunities. While often times continuing education opportunities are more geared for middle-level managers, faculty leaders, and the like, leaders need to look more carefully for such suitable opportunities. As a college and denominational leader, I didn't necessarily look for continuing education experiences aimed at CEOs. I was content to forsake my title and learn among other practitioners—a valuable exercise to understand some of the challenges faced by those who followed me as workers and to get a grasp on the trends being predicted. In addition, one of the professional organizations we belonged to as a denomination would hold an annual gathering for chief executives of denominations. The agenda only came to be only when we all arrived, ensuring the topics were those we were wishing to delve into; the learning came from the colleagues in the circle. It was always an important time of learning from others.

Third, the Johari window, especially the second pane, can be accessed in more dynamic ways instead of just by performance evaluations. Sometimes leaders complain that theirs is a lonely role. That's often true, but it doesn't need to be an isolated role without feedback and critique. Higher education uses advisory boards and other types of panels more than other organizations and workplaces, but I think they are important for leaders. Such groups allow those outside the organization to come inside and provide valuable insights and suggestions. While such groups are often called upon to evaluate programs, prepare for an accreditation visit, or better calibrate college student preparation to workplace demands, listening carefully helps the leader find feedback important for him or herself between the lines. For such groups not only address what should be done, but also how things should be done. It's the *how* which can provide important feedback and cues to the leader.

Thus, a leader follows the group to which he or she is accountable, learning to follow better the organizational mission while leading implementation of goals and strategies by engaging in self-evaluative processes, pursuing continuing education opportunities (remember the earlier characteristic of *knowledge seeking*?), and inviting outsiders in for critical and objective assessment.

Concluding Reflections

As I look back on my career journey, I often say that I was vocationally confused: first a special education-teaching principal, then a pediatric psychologist, then with a series of positions in the academic affairs area of higher education, then a college president, and finally a denominational chief executive. If that's a pathway, it has twists and turns like a switchback mountainside road!

During these twists and turns, I was asked from time to time if I had a mentor. While I never officially had a specific mentor, at many of these stops I benefitted from an older and wiser leader. I remember well times of leaning back in chairs—particularly with two different individuals—listening to their stories, stories that provided lessons for the journey. I recall one time with the university's provost when I was dean for instruction, we were talking about the financial monitoring and management that seemed to be a nuisance factor for many in academia. I asked his opinion whether I should seek a master's in business administration degree. The long answer he gave explained how he mastered the financial role as provost; the short answer was "you'll figure it out, Steve."

If a mentoring relationship presents itself, grab it. Those are the best kind. But if needed, seek one out. I have seen many younger mid-level leaders using a career coach. What a great opportunity—to learn to follow better and lead better through the eyes and wisdom of a third party.

A final word of wisdom. If you are on a clear career pathway, follow by holding on to the handrails, always moving forward. However, remember, this kind of following is like using a map to arrive at your destination. It requires confidence that the

Followership

destination is that to which you fully feel called. Yet, be sure to make room for taking detours or side trips—opportunities that often provide unexpected insights and learnings. And finally, take time to pause, reflect; pull over and enjoy the moment. Understanding and growing into a career is not a race.

Before we leave this topic, we should address filling leadership positions. While this topic is broad, I want to focus on only one dimension: appointing leaders who are women and/or members of ethnic minority groups. We've already looked at the roles gender and culture play in leadership as well as in those who follow. Further, I've also mentioned the necessity of a heterogeneous leadership group. In my relatively short six years as a denominational leader, we had approximately eight key leadership positions open up. Two positions were filled by males of European descent, one was filled by a Native American woman, another was filled by a Korean American woman and in another instance an Asian Canadian male was appointed. For two others, African American males were appointed, and we welcomed a Canadian woman of European descent to the final position.

These appointments made my heart sing! And while I was usually not hands-on involved in the searches (most often meeting the candidate as a single nominee or meeting two finalists), I found the wisdom of the director of diversity at the college I served to be key: ensure that the pool of candidates is diverse. While there are always pressures to simply move up the assistant or use word-of-mouth, such efforts don't always lead to women and/or ethnically-culturally diverse leaders. Thus, search committees were required (by previous institutional commitments) to search broadly, and I even took part in contacting prospective women and ethnic leaders to join the pool in a handful of instances. And just as a reminder, these various leaders served to lead those in their divisions and departments well, particularly as followers received new opportunities to see someone that looked like themselves or to learn how to follow patterns not springing from traditional white males.

6

Following the Leader

In Marriage and Family Life

How many of us have looked forward to our wedding days with naivete and excitement, nearly completely unaware of what marriage is all about. If you've been married more than a day or two, you already know the sky isn't always blue in our marriages. So how does a couple navigate their way throughout a marriage—especially when there is turbulence and challenges?

For believers, the age-old issue of headship can seemingly solve the challenge: the man is in charge and if the wife follows dutifully along, all will be well. Of course, this is too simple in at least two ways.

First, headship in the Bible doesn't simply refer to who is in charge. Ephesians 5:25 casts this instruction as a mirror of how Christ loves: "Husbands, love your wives, just as Christ loved the church and gave himself up for her." The instruction speaks of sacrificial love. And once we understand the basis needs to be sacrificial love, then we can begin to understand verses 22–24: "Wives, submit yourselves to your own husbands as you do to the LORD. For the husband is the head of the wife as Christ is the head of the church, his body, of which he is the Savior. Now as the church submits to Christ, so also wives should submit to their husbands in everything."

The relationship needs to be founded on sacrificial love. Second, the instruction to submit is a simile since it uses the word *as* to make a comparison. For example, to be as brave as a lion doesn't mean someone becomes a lion. Rather, it means that the person should or is taking on the characteristics of bravery as evident in a lion.

If we're to take on the characteristics of the church's submission to Christ, then we have to understand this. First of all, what it isn't. I don't know about you, but I've never seen Christ strike the church, bark at the church, or demean the church. Clearly, the loving foundation carries over to understanding these verses.

Second, the church is to follow the teaching of Christ. In marriage, the idea takes on a different form, for it's not about the wife following the teachings of her husband. Rather, the church seeks to live out this standard of love. So, too, a wife should seek to live out the standard of sacrificial love as we see in verse 25.

Taken together, there are two people. One seeking, albeit with human imperfection, to set the tone of sacrificial love. The other seeking, albeit with human imperfection, to follow that same tone. Think of this as a song. One starts singing and the other joins in. Together, the music soars.

I don't know whether you find this interpretation convincing, but I'm persuaded marriage needs to be like a duet. Sometimes singing along comes easily; at other times, it's hard to muster up the energy to sing. The point is that you've committed to a duet and each of you need to follow the musical score: sacrificial love.

So, rather than the headship notion being understood as the husband being in charge, the important notion is that the tone is built upon sacrificial love. Even when times are tough, the song must not die.

You may be wondering, then, who leads and who follows? My point is that together, each with responsibilities explained above, the husband and wife follow the musical score designed by Christ. Taking this metaphor even further, I believe, like two voices

Following the Leader—In Marriage and Family Life

blending in a duet, there is turn-taking. Sometimes one takes the melody while the other, the harmony. Sometimes there's even a solo voice for a few measures until the partner rejoins the song.

Let's try some real-life examples. Who should lead the finances of the household and who should follow? Remembering this is a duet, both should be engaged, but someone has to take the lead—the melody line. In our home, I take the lead since my gifts relate to budgeting. That doesn't mean that my wife is unaware in this sphere of our marriage. She follows with providing the harmony, asking key questions like "just because you say we can afford it, do we really need it?"

If one's income is sufficient, who should be the wage earner and who should stay home? I think back to a time when we had only one child and we each worked part-time. It wasn't a disaster, but it was certainly inefficient. We both had to know about the time of well-child visits to the pediatrician. We constantly had to compare schedules and who was home the next day. It was as if we were both trying to sing harmony—with no melody. I trust it can be done, but it wasn't the easiest for us.

If you are in the fortunate position to be able to live on one income—especially during the years of children—then it's a task of discernment: which one is most ready to be a stay-at-home parent and which one is most ready to join the workforce. Often, gender has its say, as the woman may feel the call of nurturing children rise above the call of employment (you might wish to review chapter two). But that's not always the case, and the availability of jobs comes into play as well.

More often, more than one income is needed. While the same kind of discernment is needed, managing the many responsibilities of home life becomes more complex. Clearly, expectations need to be clarified. Who is going to plan for and cook supper? And will it be a consistent responsibility or turn-taking? Who is going to cover when a child needs to stay home from school due to illness? The list goes on and on. But remember, this all has to be based on sacrificial love. "You stayed home from work last time when junior was sick; I'll stay home this time."

Followership

Of course, there are pitfalls. Sometimes, one of the marriage partners easily defaults to the other for leadership. While this may be an outcome of discerning and discussion, it can also be a cop-out. If he makes the decisions, he can be blamed. Such deference and subsequent passive aggressiveness is certainly the opposite of the picture I've tried to paint of a duet with times of melody and harmony in the score designed by Christ.

What happens for the really big issues that suddenly appear? Is it really best to defer to the one who will lead confidently? Let me share with you one that stepped into our marriage.

Our second biological child, Paul, was born with Down Syndrome and significant heart defects. At first blush, which one of us should take the lead looked like a toss-up: as a former special education teacher and at that point a pediatric psychologist in a rehabilitation hospital, one might have thought I would be capable to take the lead. However, particularly with issues related to heart functioning, open heart surgery and the like, Barb's nursing background made her a better leader. From solid knowledge of human anatomy to navigating the hospital systems, Barb was to be the better leader.

Such issues are not one-time events. From having open heart surgery at eight months of age to having to decide again when Paul turned thirty-five whether a second heart surgery was needed, I needed to follow Barb's lead. When he was eight months old, the kind of surgery performed on Paul was just new; more than once we were told "we don't know how long this fix will last." Then with some worrisome signs in his mid-thirties, that phrase took on new meaning for us. Sitting down with Paul's cardiologist and Barb in a medical consultation room back in 2021 may have left me as a third wheel, but as they talked, it was clear I needed to follow their lead as they came to the conclusion to postpone open heart surgery. Sacrificial love for Paul meant that I had to follow Barb's lead.

In all of our human imperfection, we have sought to follow—like singing a duet—the lead of each other all throughout Paul's life as we have been faced from time to time with important decisions about Paul's health. When it has come to medical issues,

Following the Leader—In Marriage and Family Life

Barb has sung the melody line with clear and pure tones. But when we have been faced with educational and vocational issues, we have taken turns with my opportunity to handle the melody line coming more frequently. While special education experts often have strong, singularly focused recommendations, we have been blessed with a variety of approaches (inclusion with regular education peers, segregated special education classrooms, job try-outs, and the like) as Paul prepared for and now functions with great independence as an adult. Most importantly, we sought to follow the Spirit's leading. Sacrificial love must be the foundation to following Christ in marriage.

What about those who are not married and have remained single? While these earlier paragraphs were written for married partners, those who are single are also called to sing. Moreover, the automatic outcome, metaphorically speaking, isn't just to provide solo work. For all—those single and those married—there are relationships with others that join in your song. Close friends, fellow church members, valued co-workers are significant. And while the single person is free to lead him or herself, to do so without accountability partners can result in troubles. Thus, like with marriage, listening well is key as your life is enriched with harmony.

I think of our life-long friend Char. Never married, but fully joined in the song with others. Char taught special education and in her last year of teaching before retirement, she had our son Paul. Following that school year, we had plans again to move to New Mexico for Barb to finish her PhD at the University of New Mexico. The previous time we had lived there, Paul was in a public school with loving and superb teachers, but the tough economic realities of that area resulted in things such as the school running out of paper, spotty math instruction, and months and months of delay in scheduling the first (and only) individual educational plan meeting. Knowing of our plans to return to New Mexico, Char offered to join us and be a personal teacher assistant to Paul. Of course we said yes, and she joined in the song with our family.

What about those with children? The same foundation is needed—sacrificial love. We also must be mindful of two key biblical

Followership

instructions. First, from Prov 22:6: "Start children off on the way they should go, and even when they are old they will not turn from it." Then, from Eph 6: 4: "Fathers, do not exasperate your children; instead, bring them up in the training and instruction of the LORD."

The key notion here is parents teaching children—in other words, leading. When children are young, the teaching is so important, for, as we learn from Proverbs, the lessons of childhood will accompany children throughout life. Also, there's a warning: don't exasperate your children. The teaching process isn't one that should lead to frustration and failure, even when as toddlers they seemingly refuse to follow. Whether it's the terrible twos or the trying times of teens, the parental role is to help children follow your lead, all the while giving them more and more room to make their own choices as they grow. At times when it may seem they are unwilling to follow, the parental response should never be to abdicate leadership. This doesn't mean at such times parents physically force followership. Rather, it's just a reminder that the best of parents don't hit a home run every time at bat. Even as you strike out in a given situation, there's the next time at bat to begin planning for. Using our song metaphor, begin planning what line you'll take on the next verse.

As a parent of seven adult children, I must readily admit the leadership/followership dynamic changes as children move into adulthood. I've had my opportunity to teach and even though I'd still like to instruct, now that they are adults, I have to step back. While I don't necessarily have to follow their leads (especially when they take the inevitable wrong turns of young adulthood), I must also remember that sacrificial love means I may have to give up a few things to continue loving them. I should give up my role of teaching parent that I had when they were young. I should give up my role of instructing them except when asked for advice. My hope, of course, is that the verse from Proverbs will come true—that they will follow Jesus, that they will learn about marriage from the many faithful models they have witnessed, that they will parent their own children in ways that the verses from Proverbs and Ephesians suggest.

Following the Leader—In Marriage and Family Life

Recently I asked our middle son, Getenet—now married with one child—what qualities or behaviors of us, his adoptive parents, would he wish to follow. His answer both surprised me and encouraged me. He said he wanted to follow our model of generosity. While in my mind the list of possibilities could be lengthy—specific approaches to child discipline, engagement in church ministry, commitment to those living on the edges of society, and the like—his answer seemed to point to Christ's sacrificial love. When we are generous, we think more of others than ourselves.

As children become adults, a curious thing begins to happen. We as parents have opportunities to follow their lead. I can think of many areas where that has already begun to happen for us. Some of our adult children have delved deeply into matters challenging the church. As such, they share their opinions, sources, and insights with us. Watching others of our adult children become parents, we have had time to reevaluate in hindsight our own practices and perspectives. More than once we have said to each other, "we shouldn't have been such uptight parents." They begin to lead the song, and we jump in, trying out new harmonies.

The dynamic flips completely when parents become elderly, requiring children to step in for decisions about when an elderly parent should stop driving, when the move into a living situation that provides assistance should occur, and ways to address a variety of medical and health issues. For the most part, our experience in this stage has been characterized by growing graciousness on the part of our parents. As my mother's health went downhill quickly before her death, she moved in with us after her final hospital discharge. She voiced her appreciation and thanks over and over as we cared for her. She followed well to the very end.

Every situation is not as sweet. When an elderly parent refuses to follow your lead and he insists on driving even when it's dangerous to him and all others on the road. When an elderly parent will not accept help even though she is unable to keep up the demands of independent living. When an elderly parent keeps ignoring health symptoms that need attention. All of these situations and more evidence the challenge it is for older parents to leave their prior roles and begin to follow the lead of their children. While there's no immediate solution for such challenges, we need to exhibit the same patience as we did as parents of toddlers: Not every time at bat results in a hit, but we need to stay in the ball game, strategizing and planning for each opportunity, and praying for grace.

In sum, we've each been called to sing the song God has called us to. For some, that might be singleness; for others, marriage. For some, without children; for others, with children. As we go through life, roles change—with sometimes dramatic changes as the end of life nears. But in any event, faithful following means no Broadway solos, no dominating the melody line to drown out the harmony. Rather, sacrificial love will provide just the right tone and sound.

Concluding Reflections

While this chapter has painted a picture nearly free from fractures and hurt, it's important to address the brokenness that can occur in marriage and family life before moving on. Borrowing from a well-known song of the early seventies, maybe this section should be called "the day the music died."

We live in a broken world and that brokenness impacts our lives. Not all marriages last. Sometimes the ending is due to unfaithfulness; other times the two individuals have grown apart in such extreme ways that there is no longer a tie that binds. Scripture puts forth the ideal for marriage and warns against adultery and other sins, so we must address life and all its brokenness against that backdrop. And if Scripture is our backdrop, we know that Christ died for our sins, giving us opportunity for renewal and restoration.

While renewal of a shattered marriage is unlikely to happen, a new marriage may be possible—a new song to sing. Moreover, we can learn something about followership in such situations. Most of the remarried people I know have mentioned their need to learn from earlier mistakes. In other words, in a previous marriage, they may have too quickly followed their impulses—to shout back, to shut out, to seek others. They have entered new marriages, committed to new ways to interact and communicate. Instead of following unhealthy patterns, they seek to learn new patterns—a new song, if you will.

Broken marriages impact children. As we've discussed, parents seek to lead children throughout the developmental journey. Shattered marriages impact these children. Their leaders (parents) become so focused on the brokenness of marriage, the children can easily be left adrift, uncertain who to follow (choosing between parents?) or what to follow (was all that stuff my parents told me phony?). In such situations, parents need to keep focus on their children as suggested by the American Academy of Child and Adolescent Psychiatry: "Children will do best if they know that their mother and father will still be their parents and remain involved with them even though the marriage is ending and the parents won't live together."[1] In other words, children still need parents to follow. Parents, despite the marital challenges, must still lead their children through this difficult time.

Finally, fractures between children and parents occur. Sometimes these broken relationships result from a specific situation but more often, specific causes are difficult to identify. What causes a young person to run away from home? Why does an adopted child reject his or her parents when entering early adulthood? Why do some parents write-off an adult child?

Such questions cause us to dig deep into topics such as early bonding, hidden trauma, and the like. Answers to these questions are as individual as each given situation. Most often they require professional assistance, and they are always complicated. Is the adopted child acting-out with her drinking and drug use due to a lack of early bonding? What about a genetic propensity to alcoholism via biological parentage? The reasons can be many and the challenges great.

I've witnessed incredible situations of grace-filled waiting. Such waiting may include some tough love (no more money, no more paid car insurance), but demonstrates love that never ends. We who are parents all long to throw a party—like the father of the prodigal son.

1. "Facts for Families," para. 7.

7

Following the Leader

In Society

PRESCHOOL AND KINDERGARTEN TEACHERS use games to teach followership. In the game Follow the Leader, one child is chosen as leader and all must follower his or her actions. In Red Light, Green Light, the child chosen to be the leader calls out the color of the light, seeking to identify those who haven't stopped for the red light in time. Learning to follow both peers and teachers is fun. Moreover, it forms an important foundation for life.

During the pandemic of the early 2020s, I was standing in a line outside a store, waiting to get in. There was a family in front of me which included parents, a girl who might have been six or seven and a boy around four. Suddenly, he darted forward, out of line, and on his way into the store before his turn. His sister, seemingly a kindergarten success story, spoke immediately to him, "Raphael, stay in line!"

Assuming most of us learned the basics of followership in kindergarten like this young girl, followership in adulthood is much more challenging than it was in kindergarten; it is considerably more complicated than a game, more challenging than simply offering easy words to say.

Following the Leader—In Society

In this chapter, understanding how and when to follow a leader is a serious topic if we're to excel at followership. In our society—particularly since the United States is a democracy—followership requires thought and intentionality. I'll begin with showcasing when followership goes awry, then include some examples of good societal followership, and then conclude by focusing on important considerations each person must address.

In the second and third decades of the twenty-first century, we've had plenty of opportunities to watch followership go awry. Of course, this is true of nearly every decade of human history. Getting followership wrong is part of the human condition, and history repeats itself over and over.

Consider what happened on January 6, 2021, when followers of then President Trump stormed the U.S. Capitol. The point in looking at this situation isn't to focus on Trump, the leader. Instead, we need to look at followership and later we'll address the dynamic of leaders and followers.

First, a quick review of what happened, as reported by NPR:

> Trump supporters, many wearing red MAGA hats but no face masks, gathered at The Ellipse where the president addressed them midday Wednesday. The crowd faced the White House and a stage was flanked by two big "Save America March" signs swayed to the beat of the Village People song "Macho Man" and Michael Jackson's "Billy Jean." After the speech, they pushed past barriers onto the Capitol grounds, while yelling, "Whose Capitol? Our Capitol," NPR's Hannah Allam reports. Police and other security put up more barriers and security layers as protesters breached the initial security layer. Protesters climbed the scaffolding, looking for any way in to get to the Capitol, Allam said, and armed police rushed in tackling them.[1]

History has already recorded the effects: defiance, destruction and even death. But the key words in the report are *after the speech*. What did the followers do? They followed with commitment,

---

1. Peñaloza, "Trump Supporters Storm," paras. 4–5.

Followership

energy, single-mindedness—pursuing what they thought their leader wanted them to do.

For some, this was the crowning event of the four years of Donald Trump followership. Leading up to and then during his presidency, Donald Trump often acted or made assertions of questionable truth, at times tinged with misogyny, racism, distrust of science, or mockery of those with disabilities. What was the impact on followers?

In general, I note three responses to Trump's presidency among his followers:

First, some were able to compartmentalize, supporting policies and his approach to government and its role, while not supporting the questionable acts or words.

Second, some looked at his leadership as a package, not willing to separate policy from pronouncements, causing them to drop their support or identification with this leader.

Third, others who also looked at leadership as a package, followed, accepting policy and pronouncements fully. And some of these became zealots as they followed their leader.

The two areas of acceptance that had significant and lasting effects are these:

COVID Pandemic

Trump downplayed the risk of COVID-19, thereby casting doubt upon medical and scientific leaders which infected the followers. A journalist, Christian Paz, listed some of these pronouncements made in the early days of the pandemic between February 7, 2020 and July 4, 2020: "The coronavirus would weaken 'when we get into April, in the warmer weather—that has a very negative effect on that, and that type of a virus,' 'It's going to disappear. One day, it's like a miracle it will disappear,' the pandemic is 'getting under control' [a claim made on July 2 when daily cases were doubling], and '99% of COVID-19 cases are 'totally harmless.'"[2]

---

2. Paz, "All the President's Lies," paras. 3–8.

Following the Leader—In Society

What were the consequences of casting doubt on the COVID-19 pandemic? Amanda Holpuch reported on a panel convened to review outcomes: "The US could have averted 40% of the deaths from Covid-19, had the country's death rates corresponded with the rates in other high-income G7 countries, according to a Lancet commission tasked with assessing Donald Trump's health policy record."[3] In other words, many followed Trump's claims and suffered from COVID and even death as a result.

Holpuch's report continued:

> In seeking to respond to the pandemic, Trump has been widely condemned for not taking the pandemic seriously enough soon enough, spreading conspiracy theories, not encouraging mask wearing and undermining scientists and others seeking to combat the virus's spread. Dr Mary T Bassett, a commission member and director of Harvard University's FXB Center for Health and Human Rights, told the Guardian: "The US has fared so badly with this pandemic, but the bungling can't be attributed only to Mr Trump, it also has to do with these societal failures."[4]

Despite these consequences, many followers accepted the mistrust of science and didn't deviate from who and how they followed, making mask wearing just one more area for political division. The BBC noted this about Americans in the early months of the pandemic:

> The wearing of masks has become a catalyst for political conflict, an arena where scientific evidence is often viewed through a partisan lens. Most Democrats support the wearing of masks, according to a poll conducted by researchers at the Pew Research Center. Most Republicans do not. The Republicans are following the lead of the president: Trump has been reluctant to wear a mask, saying that it did not seem right to wear one while he was receiving heads of state at the White House.[5]

3. Holpuch, "US Could Have Averted," para.1.
4. Holpuch, "US Could Have Averted," paras. 3–4.
5. McKelvey, "Coronavirus," paras. 4–5.

2020 Election Results Denial

The second area worthy to examine, as we look carefully at followership, is the 2020 election results. With something as large as a federal election in the US, error inevitably creeps in the gathering of results. As a society, we have learned to accept the outcomes, sometimes with second checks and recounts, ultimately trusting both the systems and the people behind the elections—no matter how close the results have been. Not so after the November 2020 election.

Donald Trump repeatedly denied the results or cast doubt on the results, making a claim on January 6, 2021 with this tweet as reported by NPR: "a sacred landslide election victory is so unceremoniously and viciously stripped away from great patriots."[6]

Did his followers adjust or did they continued to follow with denying election results? Two reactions were evident. One set of followers, whether they truly accepted the results or not, switched gears, following laws and procedures that contradicted Trump's beliefs about the election despite having had followed his lead for years. Most notable was then Vice President Pence, who wrote a letter to Congress: "It is my considered judgment that my oath to support and defend the Constitution constrains me from claiming unilateral authority to determine which electoral votes should be counted and which should not."[7]

Of course, some did not switch gears and continued to follow Trump's assessment of the election results. At the Conservative Political Action Conference (CPAC) nearly four months after the 2020 election, this report was filed: "False election claims were central to the conference, where panelists and speakers repeatedly claimed that the dead voted, that fraud changed the outcome of the election and that the American people had been sold out by everyone from the Democrats to judges to lesser Republicans."[8]

So, what do we make of the followers, both those who stormed the Capitol and others, while not part of those who were storming

6. Pederson, "Donald Trump Tweets," para.1.
7. Wise, "Pence Says He Doesn't Have Power," para. 2.
8. Timm, "Election Fraud Conspiracy Theories," para. 6.

Following the Leader—In Society

the Capitol, continued to follow Trump, accepting his leadership by refusing to wear masks and refusing to accept the 2020 election results. In other words, what can we learn about followership?

Two key factors to consider. But before we consider these factors, let me return us to my main point. All are called to followership. Those who are egocentric and those who are selfless; those who possess balanced ego-strength and those who don't; those driven to leadership and those not. And while gender and culture may also influence *how* we follow, all are called to followership, in multiple spheres of life, including politics—particularly because a democracy requires engaged citizens.

The *first factor* is to be aware of your own tendencies toward egocentrism. Without a doubt, some of Trump's followers, especially on January 6, 2021, were filled with egocentrism. Images of one of the protesters flooded the media.

Followership

It takes excessive ego strength (i.e., egocentrism) to wear such an outfit. Not only might we conclude this by his attire, but also we learned more days after the protest. This protester, Jacob Chansley, requested special organic meals while waiting in jail.[9] While not all who eat organically are egocentric, most people who eat organically don't wear horns and go around shirtless. Second, there's a correlation here between his extreme egocentrism and what he was willing to do for the leader he followed as explained by his attorney, Mr. Watkins: "Watkins has argued Chansley is not a threat to society, but instead is an *intense follower* [emphasis added] of Trump's who believed the former president had called on him to enter the Capitol building. Trump is facing a Senate impeachment trial on charges he incited the Capitol riot, and Watkins has publicly suggested that Chansley could testify during those proceedings."[10]

My hypothesis is that followers who are extremely egocentric are quickly able to follow those leaders who appeal to their self-centeredness. This is particularly true in terms of their beliefs and worldviews, thereby validating their self-image and also the unique beliefs they hold. If a person is excessively focused on their uniqueness and guarded about their diet with fears (to the point of paranoia), all out of an extreme form of self-protectionism, they may be at risk for following someone who seems to be willing to aid them in this task, offering anti-institutional perspectives and distrust of convention (including, but not limited to, scientific understanding).

Characteristic of this kind of following is that it often isn't logical. For example, it is odd that this person who is so careful about eating organically and taking care of his health isn't wearing a mask to protect himself from COVID.

In addition, such a follower, again out of egocentrism, isn't open to debate about his or her beliefs nor about the rightness or wrongness of the person they follow. Many times, we call such incredible egocentrism *radicalism*, and history is full of radicals who were so certain in their beliefs that they broke laws while they followed blindly.

9. Walsh, "'Q Shaman' From Capitol Riot," para. 1.
10. Walsh, "'Q Shaman' From Capitol Riot," para. 7.

Following the Leader—In Society

Alternatively, such extremism can be cloaked in orthodoxy—"I'm fully right and you're wrong if you don't believe what I do." Furthermore, such self-centeredness is then projected onto the leader who they follow, whether it is deserved or not. Back to Donald Trump and the oft-cited statistic that 80 percent of white evangelical Christians voted for him. Was the leader they chose a reflection of their beliefs? Probably not, given his well-known penchant for adultery, lies, and love of money. When the stock market hit thirty thousand, Trump was quoted as saying, "That's a sacred number, 30,000."[11]. But many projected upon him that which they believed and wanted to believe about him, ignoring that which didn't comport with their beliefs.

While most of us are not so egocentric that we'd dress up in horns and then demand a special diet in prison, we often tend to have selective vision—seeing what we want to see in those we follow and ignoring the rest.

The *second factor* is to be aware of your own assumptions about gender, race, and culture, recognizing these assumptions can be deeply buried. Ask any woman in leadership: "Have you ever encountered men you supervise who are dubious of your leadership?" I'm certain all would report anywhere from a few to repeated instances of this lack of followership. Why does this happen?

A generation or two ago, men were socialized to believe only men could lead and women could only follow. The husband went to work, and the wife stayed home with the kids, caring for them, making meals, and participating in volunteer activities. So, when this paradigm, as well as racial and cultural attitudes, began to shift, many men failed to change their deepest beliefs about who leads and who follows.

In society, this is made manifest explicitly as illustrated by comments like "I'll never vote for a woman president." Some see nothing wrong with the imbalance of men leaders or women leaders in Fortune 500 firms. According to a recent report "even with a record 37 female CEOs, women run just 7.4% of the 500 businesses

---

11. Zarroli, "Dow Surpasses 30,000," para. 3.

Followership

on the ranking."[12] Others, such as a political leader in the state of Michigan, referred to three women leaders—the governor, the attorney general, and the secretary of state as "witches"—saying they ought to be burned at the stake.[13] It's one thing to disagree with policies, but it's another thing to plunge to the bottom of one's own twisted assumptions and publicly voice wishes about the deaths of others.

Clearly, some men have a difficult time following women leaders in today's society. More challenging than explicit comments and actions, however, are underlying beliefs about following a woman; some would say such beliefs are buried so deep the holder of the opinion isn't even conscious of his beliefs. This kind of resistance to following a woman leader can be seen often by accompanying shielded comments. "Of course, I'd vote for a woman mayor—when the right one comes along."

Most often, however, men who dodge the chance to follow women in leadership simply fail at being advocates for such women. For such men, there's no explicit or even implicit pushback to following a woman leader; instead, it's simply unimportant and unnecessary for many to step up and advocate for women in leadership. It's no big deal.

In society, race and culture also play a significant role in resistance to following someone different from oneself. As a white male, I benefit from the privilege of good education, of having few or no stereotypes associated with my gender and race, and of being automatically part of a network of mostly men like myself. So, do I or others like me resist following those from different racial and cultural groups in today's society?

It happens. Consider the re-emergence of the Black Lives Matter slogan in 2020. While not new, the phrase reappeared after a number of senseless deaths, most notably the death of George Floyd at the hands of a police officer. Did these lives matter? For sure. Were they black men and women? Yes. Thus, it is important

---

12. Hinchliffe and McGlauflin, "Number of Female CEOs," paras. 1–3.
13. Knowles, "Michigan GOP Leader," para. 1.

Following the Leader—In Society

to emphasize that black lives matter, when society seems to be numb in response to the senseless death of black men and women.

However, many people resist endorsing this phrase and instead respond with "but all lives matter." True, all lives matter. But when a subset of the population is at risk for their very lives therefore requiring greater attention by all, it doesn't mean that other lives don't matter. Yet, there are those who refuse to follow this special emphasis, as if race doesn't matter or, worse, as if black lives are inferior.

There are other instances, too, where white folks resist following leaders of other races and cultures. Both Barack and Michelle Obama were subject to scorn that had nothing to do with policy but related only to the color of their skin. For example, in one instance, "a Kentucky Republican state House candidate is refusing to apologize for several Facebook posts depicting President Obama and the first lady as monkeys."[14]

While some people don't hold back about their feelings of not wanting to follow those racially or culturally different from themselves, we must remember two things. First, we must closely examine the deeply buried hidden beliefs we may hold. Like mentioned above, are we willing to wait "until the right racial-ethnic person comes along," never thinking that advocating for such a candidate might be our responsibility? Second, racial groups in the United States are minorities. Therefore, nearly all minority groups in the United States have had to follow a leader different from themselves and most often, white males. White folks need to learn a lesson in followership from minorities who have had to follow the lead of white mayors, community leaders of European descent, and police officers who don't look like them most of their lives.

While we must all remain vigilant against our own tendencies toward egocentrism and deeply buried assumptions about gender and culture, we should also look to examples of faithful followership in society. Consider these two, although there are many, many more:

14. Beam, "GOP Hopeful Not Sorry," para. 1.

Followership

Martin Luther King Jr. was a leader who, among other things, preached non-violence in the turbulent sixties. While today most people give him the honor and respect he is due, during the civil rights struggle, many, many white people were suspicious of him and tried to thwart his efforts. While race relations at that time boiled over into riots and all kinds of strife, looking back it is clear that King's call for non-violence was a positive influence for many of his followers. If only those with privilege would be as patient and forgiving.

A more recent example in found in the Russian invasion of Ukraine in 2022. Imagine a president—a leader—who's previous career was being a comedian! Volodymyr Zelenskyy, president of Ukraine, has provided incredible leadership—with superb skills in using all forms of media—for his people. But the key question is whether his people would follow. Indeed, they have. No stories of protests or questions about whether the Ukrainian people were willing to follow into war; Zelenskyy's approval rating in August of 2022 was at 91 percent among Ukrainians.[15]

In both of these examples, it is apparent that followership happens readily if the followers share the values of their leader. It's hard to follow a leader whose values are antithetical to yours. But it's a no-brainer to faithfully follow when values—especially bedrock values such as justice and freedom—are held in common.

Finally, recall my assertion: all are called to followership, in multiple spheres of life, including politics—particularly because a democracy requires engaged citizens. We need to turn to the Bible to better understand what God desires for engaged citizens.

The Old Testament tells the story of a theocracy, where God led, giving Israel rules to live by. Whether provided on two tablets from Mount Sinai, or throughout the first five books of the Old Testament, God's law was supreme. Are these laws still applicable to believers? As the New Testament records in Matt 5:17, Jesus explained this: "Do not think that I have come to abolish the Law or the Prophets; I have not come to abolish them but to fulfill them."

---

15. Tyshchenko, "Poll Shows," para. 1.

Following the Leader—In Society

We don't live in a theocracy. C. S. Lewis's comments in "A Reply to Professor Haldane" are instructive, especially if we are tempted to wish for such a form of government (and read the label *democrat* not as a party affiliation, but a proponent of democracy):

> I am a democrat because I believe that no man or group of men is good enough to be trusted with uncontrolled power over others. And the higher the pretensions of such power, the more dangerous I think it both to rulers and to the subjects. Hence Theocracy is the worst of all governments. If we must have a tyrant a robber baron is far better than an inquisitor. The baron's cruelty may sometimes sleep, his cupidity at some point may be sated; and since he dimly knows he is doing wrong he may possibly repent. But the inquisitor who mistakes his own cruelty and lust of power and fear for the voice of Heaven will torment us infinitely more because he torments us with the approval of his own conscience and his better impulses appear to him as temptations. And since Theocracy is the worst, the nearer any government approaches to Theocracy the worse it will be. A metaphysic, held by the rulers with the force of a religion, is a bad sign. It forbids them, like the inquisitor, to admit any grain of truth or good in their opponents, it abrogates the ordinary rules of morality, and it gives a seemingly high, super-personal sanction to all the very ordinary human passions by which, like other men, the rulers will frequently be actuated. In a word, it forbids wholesome doubt. A political programme can never in reality be more than probably right. We never know all the facts about the present and we can only guess the future. To attach to a party programme—whose highest claim is to reasonable prudence—the sort of assent which we should reserve for demonstrable theorems, is a kind of intoxication.[16]

What might fulfilling these Old Testament laws mean? That we ignore them and look only to the words of Jesus about loving God and neighbor? Tim Keller, former pastor of Redeemer

---

16. Lewis, *On Stories*, 116-117.

Followership

Presbyterian Church in New York City, poses this question and provides an answer: "Do we have reason to believe that the civil laws of Moses, although not binding, still have some abiding validity? Yes."[17]

Keller goes on to explain that the Old Testament laws reveal God's character. Focusing on justice, he suggests laws related to the care of widows, orphans, immigrants, and the poor reveal God's character: "If God's character includes a zeal for justice that leads him to have the tenderest love and closest involvement with the socially weak, then what should God's people be like?"[18]

Thus, as believers, we should yearn for these values shown in God's character and seen in Christ's fulfillment of the law. The point isn't that God's law was, is, or should be the law of the United States. I think C. S. Lewis makes that perfectly clear. The point is that believers should, in their yearning, seek civil laws that reflect these characteristics and so many more.

Therefore, it becomes a bit more clear as to who we should and should not follow in the democratic society of the United States. We should not follow those who proclaim a return to God's law. Neither should we follow those who proclaim an anything-goes, amoral society.

Both of these extremes need to be unpacked for the pluralistic society in which we live. Advancing the cause of return to prayer in the public schools, for example, could be based on the rationale that God tells his people to pray; Rom 12:12 is one of many such verses: "Be joyful in hope, patient in affliction, faithful in prayer." However, this and other calls to prayer are for believers (as well as those who do not yet believe), not for the civil laws of a nation. If we desire space for prayer in the public square and in public schools, we should give time for all to express their beliefs. Calls for abolishment of rights for those living out their same-sex attractions, a second example, can be rooted in Old Testament law. However, since we live in a New Testament era of fulfillment, those who believe these Old Testament laws translate into strict rules on

---

17. Keller, *Generous Justice*, 22.
18. Keller, *Generous Justice*, 8.

sexual behavior should direct their calls to their Christian communities, not the nation.

The second extreme, enacting an amoral society, isn't the answer either. While this postmodern era includes the notion that all truth is legitimate, regardless of the genesis of the "truth," it is impossible for a society to be based both on the rule of law and at the same time on eclectic and conflicting notions of truth. At some point, civil law needs to define right and wrong. Without such definition, society devolves into anarchy. Constitutional definitions need to be in the forefront, regardless of inherent disagreements about interpretation.

So, how should a faithful believer be engaged in society? Three guidelines. First, remember the goal isn't to re-introduce a theocracy. Instead, we live in a pluralistic society, so our goals should reflect that reality.

Second, following the characteristics of God and Christ's fulfillment of Old Testament law is all-important for a community of believers, so it is within our Christian communities that we should ask what God requires of us and grow in that knowledge.

Third, our witness, then, should be to advocate for those characteristics of God as fulfilled in Christ. For example, we should support the unborn and the born, the refugee and the poor, the widow and the orphan, the person in prison and the person just released from prison. The list goes on and on. Because all of us are called to follow faithfully, we should be following leaders who display these concerns—in their positions and in their own character—for God requires it of us. In other words, our behavior, as it reflects God's characteristics in whose image we are created, should be seen not only in what we do but in whom we follow.

Concluding Reflections

Most of this chapter focusing on followership in society has involved the examination of followership in the political realm. There are many other realms of societal following that could be addressed. In these reflections, I've selected to focus on how we all are consumers

Followership

of media—specifically the news—which is a medium by which our followership is shaped throughout these many realms.

While the media provides us reports on what's happening, the media can also be the lead platform for shaping our opinion and, at times, our behavior. Where strife has risen in recent years, governments are finding that Facebook and other social media platforms have played significant roles in shaping opinions while even instigating and leading group efforts—leading some governments to shut down the internet during such times. In the conflict Ethiopia began experiencing in 2020, Scott is one of many who have reported on the use of social media—primarily Twitter and Facebook—by both sides, each seeking to control the narrative.[19] Thus, as many in the US have learned about destruction and death in the Tigrayan region through these accounts, many Ethiopians have become frustrated with the US coming to conclusions based on what they believe is only one side of the story.

In a 1972 poll, news anchor Walter Cronkite was named as the most trusted man in America.[20] Gone are such days. Today it seems half of America gets its news from Fox, a more conservative outlet, and the other half from CNN, a more liberal outlet, with each outlet providing news (or in some cases, failing to provide news) with a not-so-secret bias. We are left uncertain as to what we should believe, wondering if we are being manipulated.

To be good followers in society, we need the news—the freedom of the press. But how can we be discerning consumers of the media in today's situation? Some of us in the United States may wish we could turn back the hands of time. Camille Caldera has summarized recent history: beginning in the late fourties, the fairness doctrine of the Federal Communications Commission required broadcasters to "'devote a reasonable portion of broadcast time to the discussion and consideration of controversial issues of public importance' and 'affirmatively endeavor to make. . . facilities available for the expression of contrasting viewpoints held by responsible elements with respect to the controversial issues,'

---

19. Scott. "How Social Media Became a Battleground."
20. Romboy, "Who Is the Most Trusted Voice," para. 1.

Following the Leader—In Society

per a report by the Congressional Research Service."[21] But during the Reagan administration, a veto ended the attempt to make this federal law. Furthermore, since it related only to the activity of granting broadcast licenses, much of today's cable new coverage would have been beyond the scope of the law.[22]

While the topic of discernment is treated more in-depth in the next chapter, I've noticed a few important things among friends and family.

First, reposting news coverage on a Facebook page is only helpful when the sharer adds discussion—even both sides of an issue—to the post. Otherwise, skip news posted on Facebook and go directly to a news source.

Second, chose news outlets that are rated to be the least biased. Ad Fontes Media publishes a chart that has both a vertical and a horizontal dimension. The vertical axis measures various media companies on a continuum from fact reporting, the strongest rating, to the opposite end of the continuum which they label contains inaccurate, fabricated info. The horizontal axis ranges from a bias to the left all the way to a bias to the right. Then with an empirical methodology, they plot the various news outlets. Outlets such as AP, Reuters, and PBS hold the spot which indicates they provide the most factual reporting and centrist perspectives. Examples of those occupying slightly lower levels—mostly because they include their own analyses with facts—are CNN (toward the left) and the *Wall Street Journal* (toward the right). Then, too, there are outlets at lower levels, on both the left and the right, that offer few facts and provide more opinions, and their reliability in reporting is variable. Examples include *Rolling Stone* of the left and *Fox News* on the right. Identifying these dimensions can be extremely helpful as one seeks to follow the news impartially.[23]

Finally, I'd recommend gathering your news from a few different sources available on the web. While sitting down and watching a complete news broadcast may seem to be the logical means

21. Caldera, "Fairness Doctrine," para. 10.
22. Caldera, "Fairness Doctrine," para. 23.
23. "Media Bias Chart 9.0."

to receive news, the result is one perspective without the opportunity for differences of opinion to creep in. Instead, scan the news on more than one website. In this way, you will get greater news coverage, differing perspectives, and you can discontinue with a click if you feel the broadcast is leading you down a rabbit hole.

8
―――――――――――

Following the Leader

In Church and Christian Community

IN THIS CHAPTER, UNDERSTANDING how and when to follow the leader in Christian community, most often a church, is another significant dimension of followership if we're to be faithful.

Christians often put their hopes and affirmations to song. For example, a favorite hymn of the Billy Graham crusades was "I Have Decided to Follow Jesus," a song that arose from the last words of the Garo martyr Nokseng:[1]

> I have decided to follow Jesus;
> I have decided to follow Jesus;
> I have decided to follow Jesus;
> No turning back, no turning back.
> Tho' none go with me, I still will follow,
> Tho' none go with me I still will follow,
> Tho' none go with me, I still will follow;
> No turning back, no turning back.

Of course, songs don't always reflect the reality of human behavior. In this chapter, understanding how and when to follow the leaders within our Christian communities is a challenging topic. We'll begin with a very brief look at leadership—and therefore,

1. "True Story behind the Song," para. 16.

followership—in Western traditions, then review how and why followership goes bad, and then end by focusing on important considerations of followership in Christian community.

The Roman Catholic tradition provides the clearest form of leadership—the Pope—and therefore, following the teachings of the church as led by the Pope gives a singularity of focus. However, within the Roman Catholic tradition, followership doesn't always mean conformity to the church. Think with me about artificial (other than natural) contraception. Although the Roman Catholic Church defines its use as wrong, many in the Roman Catholic tradition use artificial contraception, as they make their individual exceptions to the church's decrees. Another example is seen in President Joe Biden. Some say he is the most devout believer among recent presidents. Yet, there are those in the Catholic community who call him out for not following the teachings of the church.

> Archbishop Jose Gomez of Los Angeles, who heads the U.S. Conference of Catholic Bishops, praised Biden's "piety and personal story" in a lengthy statement but warned that the new president would advance moral evils and threaten human life and dignity, most seriously in the areas of abortion, contraception, marriage and gender.[2]

Henry VIII broke away from the Roman Catholic Church in 1534 and founded the Church of England, which gave rise to the Anglican communion. While the reigning monarch of the United Kingdom remains the supreme governor of the Church of England, the archbishop of Canterbury is the ecclesiastical head. In practice, then, the Anglican communion also has a clear leader to follow, although not with the infallibility associated with the Pope.

For instance, within the Church of England, the current archbishop, Justin Welby, received pushback from bishops after the release of guidelines "which said sex outside the confines of heterosexual marriage falls short of 'God's purposes for human beings'"[3] While this reporter then labeled Welby's response to

2. Dwyer and Selsky, "As Biden Prays for Healing," para. 18.
3. Nanu, "Church of England Apologises," para. 5.

the pushback as an apology, the statement issued by Welby and another said "they acknowledged 'the division and hurt' caused by their controversial guidance last week."[4] Clearly, within the church's hierarchy, as well as its membership, the authority of the Archbishop of Canterbury is not understood with the same degree of gravitas as Catholicism and the Pope.

The Reformation turned leadership upside down by focusing on Scripture as the chief source of followership. The resultant Protestantism includes a vast array of models for ecclesiastical governance, most with macro-leadership found in groups who meet in decision-making assemblies and local leadership with boards, councils, or sessions for individual congregations. While pastors are seen as leaders, authority is not theirs alone, for denominational assemblies and local church groups of elders and deacons participate in authority as well. Yet, in the Protestant world, we often see leaders operate within a seemingly unchecked independence, with the accountability springing into action only after some glaring error or controversy.

In addition to focusing on the Bible and not the Church of Rome, the Protestant tradition spawned hundreds of denominations, as a variety of biblical interpretation resulted in a variety of church bodies. Yet, ethnicity and immigration patterns shaped many of the denominations in the United States as well. Even initial names of denominations included (or still include) the founding ethnicity: Swedish Covenant, Dutch Reformed, and the Moravian Church to name a few. But, after a few generations, many of these churches began to extend beyond their initial ethnic groups.

Not only did the churches and their denominations change, the people's behavior changed as well, as denominational loyalty receded. People began to follow preachers rather than align with denominations (in their desire to follow Jesus more closely?). In many towns, cities, and villages, it was clear who the most popular preacher was. Within a denomination or even crossing over denominational lines, the best preacher in town filled the pews. Today's decreasing reliance on denominations and the rise of the

---

4. Nanu, "Church of England," para. 2.

Followership

megachurch has accentuated that tendency. Megachurches most often are built on the reputation of a single, charismatic preacher. Those that follow are often delighted in the packed pews, attributing the church's popularity to the preacher.

But we have also seen multiple occasions of leading preachers stumbling and falling. Bill Hybels (Willow Creek), Mark Driscoll (Mars Hill), and Carl Lentz (Hillsong) are a few of the more recent leaders who have had to step away from leadership. This trend isn't only seen in megachurches; parachurch organizations and higher education have seen similar failings: Ted Haggard (National Association of Evangelicals), Ravi Zacharias (Ravi Zacharias International Ministries), and Jerry Falwell Jr. (Liberty University). Not always, but often, such leadership failures result in followers leaving the church (or, in the case of other institutions and organizations, discontinuing engagement) and even leaving the faith.

Of course, leaders stumble and fall in churches with a denominational identity as well. While often not as public nor impacting as many people, impacts can be the same. In both cases, however, the issue often relates to the unchecked independence of a leader—often with followers unaware of inner workings and failures. Denominations often have mechanisms—either used well or ineffectively—to deal with leaders who stumble; megachurches require boards to rise to these challenges.

While more weighty responsibility lies with the leader and those to whom the leader is accountable, our focus is on those who follow. To aid our understanding, we should examine both myth and science.

"In the 1958 academy award-winning Disney documentary called *White Wilderness*, dozens of lemmings are shown tumbling down a cliff, bouncing off rocks and landing in the sea, where they struggle against the waves."[5] The warning is that we should be careful not to blindly follow the group. As compelling as this image has been, the event was staged and is not the behavior of lemmings. Yet, there is truth in the warning.

---

5. Fessenden, "Lemmings," para. 4.

Following the Leader—In Church and Christian Community

Studies from social psychology may better explain our behavior. Henderson has summarized some of the key research showing that we take our cues from those around us. For example, he notes that "likeminded people in a group reinforce one another's viewpoints."[6] He explains that in a complex world, simply following the crowd—that which is popular—allows us to function without digging deep into complexity. Similarly, he concludes that when we copy the majority's behavior, it most often is adaptive. These keys to human behavior lead, of course, to maladaptive actions as well, particularly when herd behavior leads to mob mentality.[7]

What does this mean for the Christian community? First, three things of which to be aware, given what social psychology tells us. Then, four things to look for in following Jesus within Christian community.

First, there was a day where homogeneity was championed in the Christian community. Consider the church growth days when experts suggested the way to grow a church was by getting people of similar ethnicity, socioeconomic levels, and lifestyles together. Certainly, they were relying on principles of social psychology. Swanson explained about the approach of a decade or more past: "The Homogeneous Unit Principle (HUP) was viewed positively as the rationale for starting churches of demographically similar people. This principle states that it is easier for people to become Christians when they must cross few or no racial, linguistic, or class barriers. Ideally, then, these new churches were led by pastors whose culture, class, and skin color closely matched those of their flocks."[8]

Swanson goes on to reject that principle, relying on Paul's messages to the early church: "It is this gospel that has 'brought near through the blood of Christ' those who were once divided by a 'wall of hostility.' God chose Paul, a Jew, to proclaim and demonstrate the reconciling gospel to people completely unlike himself."[9] He concludes, stating that "the power of God's atoning

---

6. Henderson, "Why People Follow the Crowd," para. 4.
7. Henderson, "Why People Follow the Crowd," paras. 17–20.
8. Swanson, "Down with the Homogeneous Unit Principle," para. 2.
9. Swanson, "Down with the Homogeneous Unit Principle," para. 9.

Followership

work through Jesus was displayed throughout the Roman Empire through the unlikely medium of a Jewish messenger and the powerful message of reconciliation through Christ. The same unlikely medium and message are needed today, and homogeneous models of church planting are ill suited for the task."[10]

Swanson is representative of many pointing to the unbiblical nature of homogeneity as a principle in church growth. The challenge is how to build Christ's church with followers of many different backgrounds, ethnicities, and life situations—all the while realizing the human tendency toward homogeneity.

The parish church may have arisen in neighborhoods of homogeneity. Not only were churches established in immigrant neighborhoods, these immigrants planted their own grocery stores, their own non-English newspapers, and even their own schools. However, some of these immigrant parish churches provide new opportunities years later as housing patterns have changed. Today, some are vibrant, diverse congregations with a keen eye to the challenges in their very neighborhood.

Edwards takes on the issue of multi-ethnic churches at a time when the racial divisions in the United States are both severe and raw. He focuses on "what we sociologists call a sociological imagination—which is, simply put, becoming aware of social patterns and habits."[11] Yes, we need to be fully aware of differences and the tendency toward homogeneity in thought and behavior. Then, with full awareness, he believes:

> Multiracial churches have a unique opportunity to confront white supremacy and work out the Good News in intimate community—not merely in theory or in principle, as an ethnically homogenous congregation might. To succeed, however, multiracial churches cannot be places where people of color are expected to sacrifice who they are to belong, where they have to accommodate white people's predilections, comfort levels, and expectations for the sake of diversity. Rather, multiracial

---

10. Swanson, "Down with the Homogeneous Unit Principle," para. 10.
11. Edwards, "Multiethnic Church Movement," para. 28.

churches are to be places where every person's belovedness is embraced and celebrated; where every person is able to come to the table with their gifts and skills as leaders and contributors to advance the Good News of Christ; and where no form of supremacy other than the supremacy of Christ reigns.[12]

Thus, the best way to be biblically focused while fighting the human tendency toward homogeneity begins with full awareness of the human tendency toward homogeneity and to faithfully and honestly work toward a biblical model of diversity with oneness in Christ, following a biblical principle where fruition is clearly evident in the book of Revelation.

Second, picking up the cross and following Jesus is neither popular nor easy. It's much easier to follow along with what's trendy. Sometimes the results aren't so bad. If it's popular to go to the gym and work out, you might follow the crowd and, as a result, improve your health. The same is true in the Christian community. If it's popular to give gifts to children of prisoners at Christmas, you might do the same and the children are blessed with gifts.

However, following the crowd in Christian community does not always bear good fruit. Consider these examples. Fellow believers—for whatever reason—may decide to shun face masks during a pandemic. You could follow the crowd and increase your chances of the virus latching onto you as well as giving it to others. Fellow believers may decide to turn down vaccines for their children and for themselves as well. You could follow this popular trend for yourself and even for your children, and you could be welcoming illness into your family and spreading it to others.

The effects of these popular trends within white evangelical Christianity don't just harm those following along. Their witness to the world is tarnished, suggesting by their behaviors and attitudes that God has no part in science. Of course, their hypocrisy may show, as they might very well take an antihistamine for their allergies, receive a spinal block during delivery of a child, eat

---

12. Edwards, "Multiethnic Church Movement," para. 49.

genetically engineered corn, or use medical and hospital resources when they contract the COVID virus.

This trend of following what's popular can sink deeper into the church as well. Think with me of worship. Ask yourself what components of worship in your church are derived from the Bible and what is borrowed from popular, secular gatherings or events. Ask yourself whether fog machines transform worship or simply follow the trends of the secular music industry. Raise this question: Is it worship renewal to stand jumping up and down while you worship, or does this simply mirror behavior at a rock concert? To be fair, also ask yourself whether staid, pew sitting, never moving parishioners reflect godly worship, or if this is simply behavior carried over from the prim Victorian age of generations past?

In all of these cases, what the world finds popular creeps into the attitudes and behaviors of believers, as they begin to follow other gods, just as the Old Testament children of Israel began to worship Baal. Moreover, the church and its witness is harmed. Those on the outside are able to continue to reject the faith with razor sharp discernment.

Third, I've seen believers jump from church to church, following whatever is popular at the moment. As they do so, I wonder if they have failed to think their way through these actions. Be assured, the journey of faith requires the whole person: the emotional or affective side of the person, the cognitive or thinking part of the person, and yes even the physical aspects of the person. Blended together, spirituality is balanced.

So, if the popular place to worship in town practices infant baptism and you've understood Scripture to emphasize believer baptism, does it not matter if you follow the crowd? What if the popular church you've started attending has tons of missionaries who they send far and wide, but no local diaconal program. Have you thought about that? What if the popular congregation in town flies the flag of progressiveness (or conservatism); have you thought beyond these popular positions that the church might take? Are they backed-up biblically?

Following the Leader—In Church and Christian Community

Scripture tells us in Rom 12:2 that part of our journey of sanctification requires this advice: "Do not conform to the pattern of this world, but be transformed by the renewing of your mind. Then you will be able to test and approve what God's will is—his good, pleasing and perfect will."

This can be challenging work. It's easier to follow the crowd and avoid thinking through things carefully. Why? Keeping our minds engaged can cause us to go a different way—instead of following the crowd. We may be led to take the road less traveled in our faith. Maybe that means becoming a member of a church of those unlike yourself, but because of its emphasis on the whole gospel, you know it's the best expression of faithfulness you can make.

Keeping our minds engaged can also bring us to uncomfortable places—places where the answers may not be clear. Perhaps that uncomfortable place is the pew when you size up your involvement in church and realize that you need to challenge yourself to a more thoughtful walk of obedience—but that pathway isn't so clear. Keeping our minds engaged can also lead us to be a solitary voice within our given communion. Forsaking what's popular, making waves out of true conviction doesn't always lead to acceptance by others.

Yet, the verse from Rom 12 is clear. We slide into conformity to the world when we leave our minds behind. Engaging our heads as well as our hearts enables each us to continue on the road of sanctification, and sometimes it might be a lonely journey.

How then do we follow Jesus and faithfully participate in his church? Answering this question depends, in part, on where you are at on your journey.

If you are choosing a church home. Look to see whether the church follows society's emphases or the Bible's teachings. In her book *How Shall We Worship*, Marva Dawn lists opposites which she claims are *both* [emphasis added] needed for worship that is biblical:

Followership

    truth from God . . . response from God
    head . . . heart
    freshness . . . continuity with the past
    contextualization . . . universality
    new expressions . . . familiarity for the sake of participation
    order . . . freedom in the Spirit
    joy, delight, elation . . . sorrow penitence, lament
    enthusiastic expression . . . silence
    ritual . . . spontaneity
    simplicity . . . complexity[13]

Look not only at worship, but what is also seen in the ministries of the church and its members. Of course, this is easier said than done. But be sure to dig in to understand rationale—stated reasons for ministries. If the rationale is missing, then you can be pretty sure that the church is simply following its own habits or following the crowd—secular agendas or trying to be like the church down the road. But if the rationale is present and biblical, the church in all of its human imperfection is trying to follow Jesus.

Look, too, to those in the pew. Are they at the church because they wish to be involved in following this gospel movement? Or, are they simply following their own habits or the crowd? Are they engaged in faith formative activities for themselves and others? Are they engaged in word and deed ministry? Are they seeking to serve God and neighbor before self?

You'll never find the perfect church. But hopefully you'll find a church that challenges you to continue in your own faith journey and to share the good news both for the benefit of those who do not yet believe. Find one that challenges that which sin has corrupted and is in need of God's transforming power, be it local economic structures or broader social concerns, whether it's abortion, mass incarnation, immigration, or racial injustice. Remember, your search isn't to find perfection. Rather, the goal is to join a diverse community seeking to faithfully live-out a grateful life of service to God.

---

13. Dawn, *How Shall We Worship*, 53.

Following the Leader—In Church and Christian Community

If you already are in a church home. It's important to remember that your response to God's love for you is to be a living member of a Christian community. Whether it's distrust of the institutional church or believing it's just me and Jesus, such attitudes fail to follow Jesus' teachings in so many ways. Consider Luke 4:16: "He went to Nazareth, where he had been brought up, and on the Sabbath day he went into the synagogue, as was his custom." It was Jesus' customary behavior to attend the worship service of his day. Remember, too, that Jesus gathered a group of disciples as he gave witness to the importance of groups of believers hanging together. Then there's Matthew 16:18a: "And I tell you that you are Peter, and on this rock I will build my church."

However, just because you have a church home doesn't mean that you have followership all figured out. Each and every church is a gathering of sinners. No church is perfect. Therefore, the goal we all share is that our church home helps us to be better followers of Jesus. Does the preaching help you grow in faith and understanding? Dawn digs into this question with additional questions:

> Is the public, corporate worship of our churches true to the Christian faith? Does it form its participants with the humility and wisdom of God's creation? What can we learn from nature about praising God? Does our worship enable us to be ready to die for the sake of God's glory? Does it cleanse us from our propensity to hate, hunt, hurt? Does it help us witness God's glory and nourish in us gratefulness? Wonder? Does it stir us to witness, service, adoration, fulfillment of God's purposes?[14]

Rachel Held Evans gave us, before her life ended far too early, the gift of her journey and the holy discontent she experienced in congregations as she sought to follow Jesus. While we've looked at what sometimes we mistakenly follow in our church lives, Evans introduces something she began to understand in her journey: *failure.*

> It's strange that Christians so rarely talk about failure when we claim to follow a guy whose three-year ministry was cut short by his crucifixion. Stranger still is

14. Dawn, *How Shall We Worship*, xii.

Followership

our fascination with so-called celebrity pastors whose personhood we flatten out and consume like the faces in the tabloid aisle. But as nearly every denomination in the United States faces declining membership and waning influence, Christians may need to get used to the idea of measuring significance by something other than money, fame, and power.[15]

As you consider your church home, ask yourself questions such as those Marva Dawn asked, and seek to know whether your followership is helped or hindered by your church home. Remember the goal is not success. Rather it's faithfulness.

As I write these words, our friends are struggling as they find challenges in their home congregation—a congregation that includes so many on the edges due to poverty, chronic health issues, and disabilities. While they feel they have been called to be part of this church's important ministry, the silence of their church's leadership on vaccinations has left this physician and nurse wondering about how they can follow the command to love God and neighbor, when part of the church's ministry is silent (because, as the leaders indicated, vaccines are controversial) avoiding one part of the whole person. As they began asking whether they could be faithful followers of Jesus in their church home, they eventually found a new church home where this new church home facilitates their followership of God's commands.

In sum, take joy in being part of a faith family via your church home. But if you need to ask questions about the quality of your followership, please do. You might even want to read Evan's book, *Searching for Sunday: Loving, Leaving, and Finding the Church* or C. S. Lewis if these passages lead you to wanting more:

> When I first became a Christian, about fourteen years ago, I thought that I could do it on my own, by retiring to my rooms and reading theology, and I wouldn't go to the churches and Gospel halls; . . . I disliked very much their hymns, which I considered to be fifth-rate poems set to sixth-rate music. But as I went on I saw the great merit

---

15. Evans, *Searching for Sunday*, 112.

of it. I came up against different people of quite different outlooks and different education, and then gradually my conceit just began peeling off. I realized that the hymns (which were just sixth-rate music) were, nevertheless, being sung with devotion and benefit by an old saint in elastic-side boots in the opposite pew, and then you realize you aren't fit to clean those boots. It gets you out of your solitary conceit.[16]

> For the Church is not a human society of people united by their natural affinities but the Body of Christ, in which all members, however different, (and He rejoices in their differences and by no means wishes to iron them out) must share the common life, complementing and helping one another precisely by their differences.[17]

Note in particular Lewis describes the church in its diversity. His experience probably was not one of racial diversity, but, as he says, of educational (and, I presume, socioeconomic) differences. Even if your present situation or search results in like-mindedness, there may be other important aspects of diversity that will be important for your faith journey. Moreover, such similarity of thought can lead to diverse opportunities for worship and ministry within the church and beyond when believers band together to use the multiple gifts they've been given.

Concluding Reflections

We're been in one denomination our entire lives, albeit in a variety of congregations. When we were first married, we got to know John Perkins and took his advice about the three *R*'s: Reconciliation, Redistribution, and Relocation. With respect to *relocation*, we bought our first home in a predominantly African American section of town. We explored the church within walking distance, and became members. It had originally been a

---

16. Lewis, *God in the Docks,* 61–62.
17. Lewis, *Letters,* 224

Followership

Dutch immigrant community and the church was planted there over one hundred years ago with a key purpose of worshiping in English! White flight occurred in the sixties with African Americans moving in, but the church remained, trying to shift and change during tumultuous times.

We were warmly welcomed into this church, particularly since the church had seen many more leave than join. And eventually, the first African American family joined as the church's ministry shifted more and more to its neighbors. While it didn't become a truly multiracial congregation, its sensitivity to multiculturalism continued to grow.

As I became involved in teen ministry there, one fifteen-year-old African American stood out: Brian. He was the youngest of four in a family headed by his mother. Keeping this short, he eventually moved in with us while I was able to get his mother a job where I then worked. Thus, instead of creating a divide, his mother and I grew closer as I kept her abreast of Brian's high school experiences. With three little ones in our home, Brian became an incredible big brother, including a memorable experience of driving us to the ER once when our daughter Becca severed her finger. He was a life saver in so many ways!

Brian graced our family until college graduation, and today in his fifties, is a successful entrepreneur with three daughters. He taught us much and Barb and I will always consider him part of the family. Moreover, it's important to note that Brian joined our family because of our church and its ministry. It was our first lesson in how engagement in church ministry could be life-changing as well as faith deepening.

During the pandemic of the 2020s, engagement in congregational ministry changed—but even then the Spirit was at work. Up until the pandemic, Wednesday evenings were a highlight for ministry as church member families and non-member families would come together for a meal, Bible study, and lessons and activities for the kids. While the pandemic shut this opportunity down, we adapted our ministry. For the non-member families, we created learning activities and boxed them up each week. I took some of the responsibility of delivering those boxes, stopping by the same dozen of homes (with mask on) each week. My ability to get to know these families at a deeper, more spiritual level was incredible; out of isolation and fear, true ministry occurred.

While we have hoped to model church ministry engagement to our children, for each of them the story is not yet finished. The pandemic of the 2020s has made church participation difficult for all, including each of them. We're grateful that four of our married children have chosen to be members of multiracial congregations, all small to mid-sized and situated in urban areas. Our middle son and his wife, both Ethiopian, are deciding whether to join a diverse mega-church where they would add to the diversity. Paul, our son with Down Syndrome, is at home with us, and our youngest is a book yet to be written.

As you parent, remember your words and your behavior will impact what your children do in adulthood. If you're always complaining about church, jumping from church to church, or avoiding church, your children will likely do the same. If you demonstrate not just commitment but also engagement, you will have provided your children a great model for being part of the Body of Christ. Pray that they will follow!

9

Faithful Followership

READY FOR THE FORMULA for faithful followership? Sorry, no such thing. We've looked at personality characteristics, gender, and culture and explored the challenges of following well in the transition to adulthood, in marriage and family, in work and society and in church and Christian community. Life is far too complex to end with a formula.

Yet, along the way, we've reiterated that each of us is created in the image of God, endowed with the ability to see the world around us and make sense of it. You've hopefully noted the cautions: include others with a similar worldview for your journey lest you embark on a series of missteps that will occur when you fail to see accurately. In addition, while a similar worldview is key, homogeneity in ethnicity, culture, socioeconomic status, educational level or the like isn't desirable if you are to be surrounded by the full Body of Christ.

Discernment

At times, the messages of the preceding chapters may have seemed to be that faithful followership requires a series of good decisions.

Faithful Followership

That's fair, but even better, the key task is discernment. Consider Lewis Smedes' definition:

> Seeing reality for what it is is what we call discernment. The work of discernment is very hard. Reality is always deucedly complicated; any human situation has far more to it than first meets anybody's eye. No one has twenty-twenty discernment. This is why we need other people to tell us what they see in the same chunk of reality that we are looking at. This is why people of the church need to share their visions of reality *with* each other before they shout their judgments *at* each other.[1]

Yes, discernment is hard work, and it is not a solo affair. Being among fellow believers and at church are great places to find others to assist you in this task.

Let's begin with the difficult piece. When trying to follow well, we are challenged in at least three ways.

First, for decades, psychologists have been reporting on confirmation bias, "the tendency to gather evidence that confirms preexisting expectations, typically by emphasizing or pursuing supporting evidence while dismissing or failing to seek contradictory evidence."[2] This bias not only impacts our memories and interpretations, but it relates much to social media, friendships, and even our faith.[3] It might be that in the task of discernment, one's biggest challenge is oneself! Moreover, with the ways in which the internet floods our life with information, discernment requires not only being aware of our own biases but also the disinformation (including altered images called deepfakes) that abounds in society, in our communities, and even in our churches. In one day, for example, two altered videos hit the worldwide web twenty-two days into the war in Ukraine: one in which Ukrainian President

---

1. Smedes, *My God and I*, 147.
2. "Confirmation Bias."
3. Noor, "How Confirmation Bias Works," paras. 19–24.

Followership

Volodymyr Zelenskyy is voicing surrender[4] and another in which Putin declares peace with Ukraine.[5]

Second, I trust you've noticed that following well occurs best when you don't depend only on yourself, but have relationships with others. Indeed, deep and flourishing relationships are key. However, as with all relationships, there are disruptions and challenges. Soulmates move away and you feel abandoned; your church fellowship gets embroiled in whether or not to expand the parking lot, leaving you in a spiritual drought; life becomes so crazy that there's not enough time for these relationships. Moreover, as mentioned before, it is important to have relationships with those who share similar worldviews. While we might develop relationships with those of similar *biases*, the emphasis should be on worldview—hopefully with the clarity and breadth of vision to avoid bias and assist in true discernment.

Before moving to the third factor, a cousin to relationships with people is relationships with institutions. Historically, institutions have been the foundations as well as boundaries for people whose values, beliefs, and actions need a home. Churches and denominations are institutions, political parties and neighborhood associations are institutions. Think of institutions as hyper-relationships—where people are held together in perceived unity (sometimes with great diversity) without the benefit of forming individual relationships. Today's challenge is that many, especially younger generations, are beginning not to trust these institutions. Why? Many times, these institutions are commandeered by a subgroup, wishing to champion their own beliefs instead of those the specific institution has held. The most interesting thing is that in years gone by, great conflict has enveloped these institutions when a subgroup attempts and even succeeds at imposing their will on the institution. Two examples.

We've watched the evolution of the Republican party in the US. Some would report that a more conservative subgroup has taken over the party. While some have stayed around to fight,

---

4. Allyn, "Deepfake Video of Zelenskyy," paras. 1–2.
5. Smith, "Fake Video of Vladimir Putin," paras. 1–2.

others simply have abandoned party allegiance altogether. Notice the result: the disappearance of discernment that comes with having a breadth of opinions and beliefs.

In my own denomination where we've had fifty years of addressing those with same-sex attraction pastorally, recently a subgroup organized and saw to it that the prior stance changed, drawing a dramatic line of who is in and who is out of God's love and favor. While it is too soon to tell if those opposed to this new stance will stay and challenge this change or if they will leave, already one trend is evident (especially with COVID keeping churches closed for extended periods): the younger generation is giving up on the institutional church—but not necessarily their faith or significant relationships. The church suffers, for the ability to discern together declines.

Now, a final challenge: drift. It's not only you who can't find time for these significant relationships. Your friends probably are having the same challenge. Tight during the university years, slowly this important group unravels as moves happen, jobs become demanding, and home life exerts its centrality. Again, making a decision to prioritize is so very important.

Up to this point we've talked about the necessity of these relationships for discernment and the challenges. Next, we need to discuss *how* discernment should work with you and these significant others.

What would Jesus do? A question popularized a number of years back and found on bracelets and bumper stickers. Much of this question is right on. How to live a discerning life of followership (as well as leadership) means asking oneself questions. What would Jesus do? Would he hang-out with sinners, show compassion to those on the edges, teach through stories? Indeed. Yet, this can't be our only question.

Jesus' disciples, many who were the inspired authors of the New Testament books, not only told us what Jesus did, but through the work of the Holy Spirit, grouped incidences together so we could better understand. For we learn not only from what Jesus *did*, but we are also given the pronouncements he made, the stories he told, and the questions he asked. Take a look at Luke 6. First, we are led to understand more about the deep meaning of the Sabbath by a couple of stories, ending with Jesus' question in the ninth verse: "I ask you, which is lawful on the Sabbath: to do good or to do evil, to save life or to destroy it?"

Next in Luke 6, Jesus echoes words found in Matthew's account of the Beatitudes. This time, Jesus adds the counter point in verses 24–26, each statement beginning with: "Woe unto you who . . ." followed by a warning.

Then Luke provides two sections on Jesus' instructions about loving enemies and judging others and concludes this chapter by providing two images—one of a tree and its fruit and one of a builder.

Indeed, our question in the process of discernment cannot only be "what did Jesus do?" Luke 6 is just one of many chapters that is rich with the words and stories of Jesus. We also must ask "what did Jesus teach?"

Paul, although not one of the original disciples, takes what Jesus did and what Jesus taught and expounds upon it for our benefit. In Romans, for instance, he explains Christ's coming, death, and resurrection in a way that we learn more about salvation, grace, justification, sanctification, and a whole bunch more. In his first letter to the Corinthians, Paul is addressing those in a cosmopolitan and immoral city and explaining how to live a holy life and includes an emphasis upon spiritual gifts, the greatest of which is love.

Further, just as Paul references the Old Testament, we, too, need to rely on the Old Testament along with the New Testament to discern more fully. While sometime the instructions in the Old Testament are more nuanced (e.g., needing to understand the historical context), at other times they are fairly simple to understand. Micah 6:8 provides us a bedrock instruction for discerning how to live and who and what to follow: "He has shown you, O mortal, what is good. And what does the LORD require of you? To act justly and to love mercy and to walk humbly with your God."

Faithful Followership

Notice, too, we must encounter the Trinity—Father, Son, and Holy Spirit. It's not only about what Jesus would do. It's about what God created, for example. Understanding how to appreciate our climate should bring us back to Genesis. God created the world good. Genesis 1:31 says this: "God saw all that he had made, and it was very good." Not an instruction, but a starting point for the question we need to ask ourselves as we decide how to follow science and public opinions relative to climate change.

We also find in the creation story the related concept of caretaking. Genesis 2:15: "The Lord God took the man and put him in the Garden of Eden to work it and take care of it." What does that mean for us? What and whom do we follow to not only individually but societally care for the earth? Do we follow those who promote a return to coal for our energy source or those who promote solar power? Do we follow a reliance on gas-powered vehicles or electric vehicles?

Finally, both in terms of our analysis here and for the conclusion of this book, we look to the Holy Spirit for discernment. Colossians 3:14 states "And over all these virtues put on love, which bind them all together in perfect unity." How do we do this? Through the power of the Holy Spirit working in us. Putting on love—in all things, and even in our discernment of who and what to follow.

First Corinthians 13 provides a wonderful set of examples of the need for love, with examples like that found in verse 3: "If I give all I possess to the poor and give over my body to hardship that I may boast, but do not have love, I gain nothing." And then immediately following this chapter, the next chapter begins by pointing to the source of love: "Follow the way of love and eagerly desire gifts of the Spirit . . ."

Servanthood

While the first part of this chapter has dealt with biblical discernment that requires community, the final part of this chapter focuses

Followership

on servanthood. Just as many have explored servant *leadership*, so too should we explore servant *followership*.

Greenleaf is credited with being the founder or definer of servant leadership. Consider his explanation:

> The servant-leader *is* servant first. . . . It begins with the natural feeling that one wants to serve, to serve *first*. Then conscious choice brings one to aspire to lead. That person is sharply different from one who is *leader* first, perhaps because of the need to assuage an unusual power drive or to acquire material possessions. . . . The leader-first and the servant-first are two extreme types. Between them are shadings and blends that are part of the infinite variety of human nature. The difference manifests itself in the care taken by the servant-first to make sure that other people's highest priority needs are being served. The best test, and difficult to administer, is: Do those served grow as persons? Do they, *while being served*, become healthier, wiser, freer, more autonomous, more like themselves to become servants? *And*, what is the effect on the least privileged in society? Will they benefit or at least not be further deprived?[6]

Others have focused on dimensions of servant leaders:

> *Valuing People.* Servant leaders value people for who they are, not just for what they give to the organization. Servant leaders are committed first and foremost to people—particularly, their followers.
>
> *Humility.* Servant leaders do not promote themselves; they put other people first. They are actually humble, not humble as an act. Servant leaders know leadership is not all about them—things are accomplished through others
>
> *Listening.* Servant leaders listen receptively and nonjudgmentally. They are willing to listen because they truly want to learn from other people and to understand the people they serve; they must listen deeply. Servant leaders seek first to understand, and then to be understood.

---

6. Greenleaf and Spears, *Power of Servant-Leadership*, 123.

Faithful Followership

This discernment enables the servant leader to know when their service is needed.

Trust. Servant leaders give trust to others. They willingly take this risk for the people they serve. Servant leaders are trusted because they are authentic and dependable.

Caring. Servant leaders have people and purpose in their heart. They display a kindness and concern for others. As the term *servant leadership* implies, servant leaders are here to serve, not to be served. Servant leaders truly care for the people they serve.[7]

Translating servant *leadership* into servant *followership*, the test Greenleaf offers in his definition (see above) is valuable, and revised slightly to fit it to followership: *Are those who follow growing as persons? Are they becoming healthier, wiser, freer, more autonomous, more like themselves to become servants?*

What might this mean? Perhaps a servant follower is quick to serve the leader: with allegiance sprinkled with discernment (chapter five introduced the *Star Follower* and *Partner*), with gifts of completed assignments and productivity and with the added value of personal creativity—all with cheerfulness embedded with thoughtfulness. Does such a follower become more healthy, wise, free, more autonomous and more like themselves?

In addition, a servant follower is not only attentive to the leader. A servant follower is attentive to fellow followers, those following with rapt attention as well as those lagging behind (again, recall chapter five and the introduction of the *Disciple*). For both, the servant follower encourages others while seeking to understand their contexts, challenges, and concerns; assists others while promoting independence, not co-dependence; thinks less of him or herself and more of the others which may include denying self until the needs of others are met; meeting the ideas and pronouncements of others with humility; and practicing acceptance as fellow image-bearers of God.

---

7. Witt, "Top 5," para. 3.

Followership

Maybe the concept of a servant follower is unnecessary, or maybe it's the tip of an iceberg. Regardless of your reaction, allow me to end with some personal reflections.

After forty-two years of marriage and living out of a shared biblical worldview, Barb and I have pursued or followed God's lead in ways that mirror the values he has given us. For many years, we lived in the central city, developing relationships with those on the edge of poverty and most often African Americans. I've mentioned some of these stories before. In addition, at some point we decided on a goal to double our tithe. That action has led to all kinds of rewards, from helping provide scholarship dollars to international students, to giving a car away to benefit a local school, and supporting faith-based charities that reflect our values.

Our adoption of three siblings from Ethiopia who lost their parents changed our life. We learned to follow different scripts and new patterns as together we navigated differing cultural patterns. Our cross-cultural values multiplied and our relationships with others with similar experiences deepened. Rather than storehousing resources in this stage of life, we invested fully into the lives of our children, ensuring college was possible, family time was important, and service was modeled.

Helping our middle son start a Christian special education school in Ethiopia came naturally as did serving in a summer camp program for urban families headed by single parents. Having numerous college students who were short on finances live with us for a summer or longer over the years has been commonplace, and Barb's doctoral studies in health promotion on the Navajo reservation was a beneficial stretch for all of us.

In short, we have sought to follow God's lead, from our earliest days as a married couple (Barb was twenty-one and I was twenty when we married), always digging deeper into our shared worldview and its biblical foundation—most often in small groups or in church, and refining our values and behaviors to put God first, neighbors second, and ourselves last.

Of course, we've had challenges and difficulties. I think this present season of disinformation coupled with confirmation bias

Faithful Followership

is one of the most difficult. Whether it's the flood of disinformation about government, beliefs about health measures during a pandemic, or divisions in the church, following well can lead to misrepresentations others have of you, loss of friendships, and even church exits.

Yet, wherever you are on your journey of followership, look forward. The things I just mentioned didn't rain down on us while we were twenty-somethings. No, these stories involve a lifetime of following God, discerning each step of the way while listening to the wise voices God placed in our workplaces, congregations, and communities—regardless of the specific season that provides our various contexts. May your journey of followership be as blessed as ours has been.

In closing, we should reflect on the words of Justin Welby, the Archbishop of Canterbury (Church of England) given at the funeral of Queen Elizabeth II: "Jesus—who in our reading does not tell his disciples how to follow, but who to follow—said 'I am the way, the truth and the life.' Her late Majesty's example was not set through her position or her ambition, but through whom she followed."[8]

---

8. Sachdeva, "We Will Meet Again," para. 7.

Bibliography

Abcarian, Robin. "Michelle Obama's Stunning Convention Speech: When They Go Low, We Go High." *Los Angeles Times*, Jul 25, 2016. https://www.latimes.com/politics/la-na-pol-michelle-speech-20160725-snap-story.html.

"Agentic State." *APA Dictionary of Psychology*. https://dictionary.apa.org/agentic-state.

Allyn, Bobby. "Deepfake Video of Zelenskyy Could Be 'Tip of the Iceberg' in Info War, Experts Warn." *NPR*, Mar 16, 2022. https://www.npr.org/2022/03/16/1087062648/deepfake-video-zelenskyy-experts-war-manipulation-ukraine-russia.

Badger, Emily. "Michelle Obama on Being Black: There Will Be Times When You Feel Like Folks Look Right Past You." *Washington Post*, May 11, 2015. https://www.washingtonpost.com/news/wonk/wp/2015/05/11/michelle-obama-on-the-invisibility-of-being-black-in-america-today/.

Beam, Adam. "GOP Hopeful Not Sorry for Posts Depicting Obamas as Monkeys." *Associated Press*, Sep 30, 2016. https://apnews.com/article/90ec82dfca4f45e48628e4ae45b8247f.

Buchanan, Leigh. "Inside the Mind of the Entrepreneur." *Inc.*, Sep 2014. https://www.inc.com/magazine/201409/leigh-buchanan/inc.500-introduction-to-the-2014-winners.html.

Caldera, Camille. "Fact Check: Fairness Doctrine Only Applied to Broadcast Licenses, Not Cable TV Like Fox News." *USA Today*, Nov 28, 2020. https://www.usatoday.com/story/news/factcheck/2020/11/28/fact-check-fairness-doctrine-applied-broadcast-licenses-not-cable/6439197002/.

Chaleff, Ira. *Courageous Follower: Standing Up to and for Our Leaders*. Oakland: Berrett-Koehler, 2009.

Coggins, Eric. "Three Top Models of Courageous Followership." *Tough Nickel*, Jun 2020. https://toughnickel.com/business/Leadership-in-the-21st-Century-Theories-of-Courageous-Followership.

Bibliography

"Confirmation Bias." *APA Dictionary of Psychology.* https://dictionary.apa.org/confirmation-bias.

Dawn, Marva. *How Shall We Worship? Biblical Guidelines for the Worship Wars.* Wheaton, IL: Tyndale House, 2003.

Du Mez, Kristin Kobes. *Jesus and John Wayne: How White Evangelicals Corrupted a Faith and Fractured a Nation.* New York: Liveright, 2020.

Dwyer, Devin, and Lauren Selsky. "As Biden Prays for Healing, Catholics Clash Over President's Faith." *ABC News*, Feb 1, 2021. https://abcnews.go.com/Politics/biden-prays-healing-catholics-clash-presidents-faith/story?id=75546190.

Edwards, Korie Little. "The Multiethnic Church Movement Hasn't Lived up to its Promise." *Christianity Today*, Feb 16, 2021. https://www.christianitytoday.com/ct/2021/march/race-diversity-multiethnic-church-movement-promise.html.

Eggert, David. "Michigan State Police Disproportionately Stop Black Drivers." *Detroit Free Press*, Jan 12, 2022. https://www.freep.com/story/news/local/michigan/2022/01/12/state-police-disproportionately-stop-black-drivers/9196046002/.

"Ego Strength." *APA Dictionary of Psychology.* https://dictionary.apa.org/ego-strength.

Evans, Rachel Held. *Searching for Sunday: Loving, Leaving, and Finding the Church.* Nashville: Nelson Books, 2015.

"Facts for Families: Children and Divorce." American Academy of Child and Adolescent Psychiatry, Jan 2017. https://www.aacap.org/AACAP/Families_and_Youth/Facts_for_Families/FFF-Guide/Children-and-Divorce-001.aspx.

Fessenden, Maris. "Lemmings Do Not Explode or Throw Themselves Off Cliffs." *Smithsonian Magazine*, Nov 26, 2014. https://www.smithsonianmag.com/smart-news/lemmings-do-not-explode-or-throw-themselves-cliffs-180953475/.

Fording, Richard, and Sanford Schram. *Hard White: The Mainstreaming of Racism in American Politics.* Oxford: Oxford University Press, 2020.

Garber, Steven. *The Fabric of Faithfulness: Weaving Together Belief and Behavior During the University Years.* Downers Grove: InterVarsity, 1996.

Gino, Francesca, and Alison Wood Brooks. "Explaining Gender Differences at the Top." *Harvard Business Review*, Sept. 23, 2015. https://hbr.org/2015/09/explaining-gender-differences-at-the-top.

Greenleaf, Robert, and Larry Spears. *The Power of Servant-Leadership: Essays.* Oakland: Berrett-Koehler, 1998.

Grijalva, E., et al. "Gender Differences in Narcissism: A Meta-Analytic Review." *Psychological Bulletin* 141 (2015) 261–310. https://doi.org/10.1037/a0038231.

Hanson, Kait. "Serena Williams Says She Had to Choose between Motherhood and Tennis." *Today*, Aug 9, 2022. https://www.today.com/parents/parents/serena-williams-retires-tennis-motherhood-rcna42201.

Bibliography

Henderson, Rob. "The Science Behind Why People Follow the Crowd." *Psychology Today*, May 24, 2017. https://www.psychologytoday.com/us/blog/after-service/201705/the-science-behind-why-people-follow-the-crowd.

Henriques, Gregg. "The Relationship Styles of Men and Women." *Psychology Today*, Sep 11 2013. https://www.psychologytoday.com/us/blog/theory-knowledge/201309/the-relational-styles-men-and-women.

Hinchliffe, Emma, and Paige McGlauflin. "The Number of Female CEOs in the Fortune 500 Hits an All-Time Record." *Fortune*, May 18, 2020. https://fortune.com/2022/08/03/number-of-female-ceos-running-global-500-companies-hits-record-high/.

Holpuch, Amanda. "US Could Have Averted 40% of Covid Deaths, Says Panel Examining Trump's Policies." *The Guardian*, Feb 11, 2021. https://www.theguardian.com/us-news/2021/feb/10/us-coronavirus-response-donald-trump-health-policy.

Jabr, Ferris. "The Neuroscience of 20-Somethings." *Scientific American*, Aug 29, 2012. https://blogs.scientificamerican.com/brainwaves/the-neuroscience-of-twenty-somethings/.

Keller, Tim. *Generous Justice: How God's Grace Makes Us Just*. London: Penguin Books, 2010.

Kelly, Robert. *The Power of Followership*. New York: Doubleday, 1992.

Knowledge at Wharton Staff. "How Cultural Factors Affect Leadership." July 23, 1999. http://knowledge.wharton.upenn.edu/article/how-cultural-factors-affect-leadership/.

Knowles, Hannah. "Michigan GOP Leader Calls Top Democrats 'Witches,' Jokes about Assassination of Republicans." *Washington Post*, Mar 27, 2021. https://www.washingtonpost.com/politics/2021/03/27/ron-weiser-michigan-witches-assassination/.

Lewis, C. S. *God in the Dock: Essays on Theology and Ethics*. Grand Rapids: Eerdmans, 1970.

———. *On Stories and Other Essays on Literature*. New York: Harper Collins, 1982.

———. *Letters of C. S. Lewis*. Warren Hamilton Lewis, ed. New York: Harcourt, Brace, World, 1966.

Ludeman, Kate, and Eddie Erlandson. "Coaching the Alpha Male." *Harvard Business Review*, May 2004. https://hbr.org/2004/05/coaching-the-alpha-male#:~:text=Bold%2C%20self%2Dconfident%2C%20and,also%20drive%20their%20coworkers%20crazy.

Martinez, A., and Tom Dreisbach. "A Son Takes the Stand against His Father in the First Trial Related to Jan. 6 Riot." *NPR Morning Edition*, Mar 4, 2022. https://www.npr.org/2022/03/04/1084448605/a-son-takes-the-stand-against-his-father-in-the-first-trial-related-to-jan-6-rio.

McKelvey, Tara. "Coronavirus: Why Are Americans So Angry about Masks?" *BBC*, Jul 20, 2020. https://www.bbc.com/news/world-us-canada-53477121.

Bibliography

"Media Bias Chart 10.0." Ad Fontes Media, Jan 2020. https://adfontesmedia.com/static-mbc/?utm_source=HomePage_StaticMBC_Image&utm_medium=OnWebSite_Link.

Nanu, Maighna. "Church of England Apologises for Saying Sex Is Just for Married Heterosexuals." *Independent*, Jan 31, 2020. https://www.independent.co.uk/news/uk/home-news/church-england-sex-lgbt-gay-marriage-justin-welby-apology-a9310811.html.

Noor, Iqra. "How Confirmation Bias Works." *Simply Psychology*, Jun 10, 2020. www.simplypsychology.org/confirmation-bias.html.

Paz, Christian. "All the President's Lies about the Coronavirus." *The Atlantic*, Nov 2, 2020. https://www.theatlantic.com/politics/archive/2020/11/trumps-lies-about-coronavirus/608647/.

Pedersen, Erik. "Donald Trump Tweets about 'Sacred Landslide Victory' after Telling Protesters to Go Home but Adding 'We Love You'—Update." *Deadline*, Jan 6, 2021. https://deadline.com/2021/01/donald-trump-speech-capitol-protest-go-home-election-was-stolen-1234666061/.

Peñaloza, Marisa. "Trump Supporters Storm US Capitol, Clash with Police." *NPR*, Jan 6, 2021. https://www.npr.org/sections/congress-electoral-college-tally-live-updates/2021/01/06/953616207/diehard-trump-supporters-gather-in-the-nations-capital-to-protest-election-result.

Plantinga, Cornelius. *Engaging God's World: A Reformed Vision of Faith, Learning, and Living*. Grand Rapids: Eerdmans, 2002.

Poleacovschi, Cristina, et al. "Gendered knowledge accessibility: Evaluating the role of gender in knowledge seeking among engineers in the US." *Journal of Management in Engineering* 37.1 (Sep 2021) 1–10.

Ray, Rashawn, and Alexandra Gibbons. "Why Are States Banning Critical Race Theory?" Nov 2021. https://www.brookings.edu/blog/fixgov/2021/07/02/why-are-states-banning-critical-race-theory/.

Riggo, Ronald, et al. *The Art of Followership: How Great Followers Create Great Leaders and Organizations*. San Francisco: Jossey-Bass, 2008.

Romboy, Dennis. "Who Is the Most Trusted Voice in America?" *Deseret News*, Jan 9, 2021. https://www.deseret.com/utah/2021/1/9/21542674/trusted-voice-america-bill-gates-oprah-obama-dolly-parton-taylor-swift-tom-hanks.

Rovelli, Paola, and Camilla Curnis. "The Perks of Narcissism: Behaving Like a Star Speeds Up Career Advancement to the CEO Position." *Leadership Quarterly*, 34.3 (Jun 2021) 1–13. https://www.sciencedirect.com/science/article/pii/S1048984320301168.

Ryan, Liz. "Ten Unmistakable Signs of a Toxic Culture." *Forbes*, Oct 19, 2016. https://www.forbes.com/sites/lizryan/2016/10/19/ten-unmistakable-signs-of-a-toxic-culture/?sh=1ce66e50115f

Suchdeva, Rhythm. "'We Will Meet Again': Read the Archbishop of Canterbury's Full Sermon at Queen's Funeral." *CTV News*, Sep 19, 2022. https://www.ctvnews.ca/world/we-will-meet-again-read-the-archbishop-of-canterbury-s-full-sermon-at-queen-s-funeral-1.6074113.

Bibliography

Scott, Liam. "How Social Media Became a Battleground in the Tigray Conflict." *Voice of America*, Oct 17, 2021. https://www.voanews.com/a/how-social-media-became-a-battleground-in-the-tigray-conflict-/6272834.html.

Smedes, Lewis. *My God and I: A Spiritual Memoir*. Grand Rapids: Eerdmans, 2003.

Smietana, Bob. "Josh McDowell Steps Back from Ministry after Race Remark." *Christianity Today*, Sep 23, 2021. https://www.christianitytoday.com/news/2021/september/josh-mcdowell-race-comments-ccaa-step-down-ministry.html.

Smith, Adam. "Fake Video of Vladimir Putin Declaring Peace with Ukraine Seeks to Cause Chaos Online." *The Independent*, Mar 19, 2022. https://www.independent.co.uk/tech/fake-video-vladimir-putin-peace-ukraine-b2039078.html.

"Social Cognition." *APA Dictionary of Psychology*. https://dictionary.apa.org/social-cognition.

Stetka, Bret. "Extended Adolescence: When 25 Is the New 18." *Scientific American*, Sep 19, 2017. https://www.scientificamerican.com/article/extended-adolescence-when-25-is-the-new-181/.

Swanson, David. "Down with the Homogeneous Unit Principle?" *Christianity Today*, Aug 2, 2010. https://www.christianitytoday.com/pastors/2010/august-online-only/down-with-homogeneous-unit-principle.html.

"The True Story behind the Song 'I Have Decided to Follow Jesus.'" *Renewal Journal*, Nov 20, 2017. https://renewaljournal.com/2017/11/29/the-true-story-behind-the-song-i-have-decided-to-follow-jesus/.

Timm, Jane. "Election Fraud Conspiracy Theories Find a Friendly Audience at CPAC." *NBC News*, Feb 28, 2021. https://www.nbcnews.com/politics/elections/election-fraud-conspiracy-theories-find-friendly-audience-cpac-n1259100.

Tyshchenko, Kateryna. "Poll Shows 98% Ukrainians Believe in Ukraines Victory, 91% Approve of Zelenskyy." *Ukrainska Pravda*, Aug 11, 2022. https://www.pravda.com.ua/eng/news/2022/08/11/7362903/.

Walsh, Joe. "'Q Shaman' from Capitol Riot Hasn't Eaten in over a Week Because Jail Won't Offer Organic Food, Lawyer Says." *Forbes*, Feb 3, 2021. https://www.forbes.com/sites/joewalsh/2021/02/03/q-shaman-from-capitol-riot-hasnt-eaten-in-over-a-week-because-jail-wont-offer-organic-food-lawyer-says/?sh=731dff554e52.

Walsh, Brian, and J. Richard Middleton. *The Transforming Vision: Shaping a Christian Worldview*. Downers Grove: InterVarsity, 1984.

Wise, Alana. "Pence Says He Doesn't Have Power to Reject Electoral Votes." *NPR*, Jan 6, 2021. https://www.npr.org/sections/congress-electoral-college-tally-live-updates/2021/01/06/953995808/pence-says-he-doesnt-have-power-to-reject-electoral-votes.

Witt, David. "The Top 5 Characteristics of Servant Leaders." *Blanchard LeaderChat*, Oct 25, 2018. https://leaderchat.org/2018/10/25/research-the-top-5-characteristics-of-servant-leaders/.

Bibliography

Zarroli, Jim. "The Dow Surpasses 30,000 for 1st time ever." *NPR*, Nov 24, 2020. https://www.npr.org/2020/11/24/938593059/the-dow-surpasses-30-00-for-1st-time-ever.

www.ingramcontent.com/pod-product-compliance
Lightning Source LLC
Chambersburg PA
CBHW070920180426
43192CB00038B/2017